BALLADS AND POEMS

ILLUSTRATING ENGLISH HISTORY

BALLADS AND POEMS

ILLUSTRATING

ENGLISH HISTORY

Edited by

FRANK SIDGWICK

CAMBRIDGE:

at the University Press

1927

CAMBRIDGE
UNIVERSITY PRESS

University Printing House, Cambridge CB2 8BS, United Kingdom

Published in the United States of America by Cambridge University Press, New York

Cambridge University Press is part of the University of Cambridge.

It furthers the University's mission by disseminating knowledge in the pursuit of education, learning and research at the highest international levels of excellence.

www.cambridge.org
Information on this title: www.cambridge.org/9781107632325

First edition 1907
Reprinted 1907, 1908, 1909, 1912, 1913, 1927
Plain text edition 1914
First published 1914
First paperback edition 2013

A catalogue record for this publication is available from the British Library

ISBN 978-1-107-63232-5 Paperback

PREFACE.

A NUMBER of the poems in this book are to be found in many similar collections of historical poems, and only the limits imposed by the law of copyright have prevented the inclusion of others, such as Tennyson's *Revenge*. It is hoped, however, that this deficiency may be more than compensated by the presence of many less hackneyed poems, and in particular of several fine ballads, some of which have hitherto not been put before young pupils. While it must be admitted that these are not conspicuous for historical fidelity, I venture to think that their literary interest is a distinct advantage for educational purposes; and a word or two of guidance to teachers who use this book may not be out of place.

Firstly, every piece is meant to be learned by heart, and half a dozen at least have tunes. Secondly, the distinctions between the "artistic" poems, the traditional ballads, and the "popular" contemporary songs, should be kept clearly in the pupil's mind. Thirdly, seeing that this mixture of styles has necessitated an arrangement by chronological order of subject-matter, each piece should be so dealt with that the pupil realises the conditions under which it was written. To this end I have added, to the notes on the "artistic" poems, short accounts of their respective authors, and have elaborated the notes on the traditional and "popular" poems and ballads. Proper handling of certain ballads will arouse interest in the methods of oral tradition. In the note to *King John and the Abbot of Canterbury* a hint, easily expanded, is given of the vogue which such folk-tales may enjoy. The poems by Hawker and Wolfe have interesting literary histories, which serve to demonstrate that "artistic" poems may occasionally undergo experiences similar to those of "popular" verse.

The best method of expounding each poem, according as it narrates, disguises, or illustrates history, will be easily decided by the teacher, who will find that the fulness or paucity of the notes is in inverse ratio to the amount of information ordinarily accessible in history-books. Etymological notes are almost entirely omitted, in the belief that interest in the growth of a language is of later development than that interest in the growth of a nation and its literature which this book endeavours to stimulate.

F. S.

January 1907.

CONTENTS.

BALLADS AND POEMS
ILLUSTRATING ENGLISH HISTORY

BOADICEA

(A.D. 61)

When the British warrior Queen,
  Bleeding from the Roman rods,
Sought, with an indignant mien,
  Counsel of her country's gods,

Sage beneath a spreading oak,
  Sat the Druid, hoary chief,
Every burning word he spoke
  Full of rage, and full of grief.

"Princess! if our aged eyes
  Weep upon thy matchless wrongs, 10
'Tis because resentment ties
  All the terrors of our tongues.

"Rome shall perish—write that word
  In the blood that she has spilt;
Perish, hopeless and abhorr'd,
  Deep in ruin as in guilt.

"Rome, for empire far renown'd,
  Tramples on a thousand states;
Soon her pride shall kiss the ground—
  Hark! the Gaul is at her gates! 20

"Other Romans shall arise,
  Heedless of a soldier's name;
Sounds, not arms, shall win the prize
  Harmony the path to fame.

"Then the progeny that springs
  From the forests of our land,
Arm'd with thunder, clad with wings,
  Shall a wider world command.

"Regions Cæsar never knew
  Thy posterity shall sway; 30
Where his eagles never flew,
  None invincible as they."

Such the bard's prophetic words,
  Pregnant with celestial fire,
Bending as he swept the chords
  Of his sweet but awful lyre.

She, with all a monarch's pride,
  Felt them in her bosom glow:
Rush'd to battle, fought, and died;
  Dying, hurl'd them at the foe. 40

"Ruffians, pitiless as proud,
  Heaven awards the vengeance due;
Empire is on us bestow'd,
  Shame and ruin wait for you."

WILLIAM COWPER.

KING CANUTE

(1020)

King Canute was weary-hearted; he had reigned for
years a score,
Battling, struggling, pushing, fighting, killing much
and robbing more;
And he thought upon his actions, walking by the
wild sea-shore.

'Twixt the chancellor and bishop walked the king with
steps sedate,
Chamberlains and grooms came after, silversticks and
goldsticks great,
Chaplains, aides-de-camp, and pages—all the officers
of state,

Sliding after like his shadow, pausing when he chose
to pause;
If a frown his face contracted, straight the courtiers
dropped their jaws;
If to laugh the king was minded, out they burst in
loud hee-haws.

But that day a something vexed him, that was clear
to old and young: 10
Thrice his grace had yawned at table, when his
favourite gleemen sung,
Once the queen would have consoled him, but he bade
her hold her tongue.

"Something ails my gracious master," cried the keeper
of the seal.
"Sure, my lord, it is the lampreys served at dinner, or
the veal?"
"Pshaw!" exclaimed the angry monarch. "Keeper,
'tis not that I feel.

"'Tis the *heart*, and not the dinner, fool; that doth my
rest impair:
Can a king be great as I am, prithee, and yet know no
care?
Oh, I'm sick, and tired, and weary."—Some one cried,
"The king's arm-chair!"

Then towards the lackeys turning, quick my lord the
keeper nodded,
Straight the king's great chair was brought him, by
two footmen able-bodied; 20
Languidly he sank into it: it was comfortably wadded.

"Leading on my fierce companions," cried he, "over
storm and brine,
I have fought and I have conquered! Where was
glory like to mine?"
Loudly all the courtiers echoed: "Where is glory like
to thine?"

"What avail me all my kingdoms? Weary am I
now and old;
Those fair sons I have begotten, long to see me dead
and cold;
Would I were, and quiet buried, underneath the silent
mould!

"Oh, remorse, the writhing serpent! at my bosom tears and bites;
Horrid, horrid things I look on, though I put out all the lights;
Ghosts of ghastly recollections troop about my bed at nights. 30

"Cities burning, convents blazing, red with sacrilegious fires;
Mothers weeping, virgins screaming vainly for their slaughtered sires."—
"Such a tender conscience," cries the bishop, "every one admires.

"But for such unpleasant bygones, cease, my gracious lord, to search,
They're forgotten and forgiven by our Holy Mother Church;
Never, never does she leave her benefactors in the lurch.

"Look! the land is crowned with minsters, which your grace's bounty raised;
Abbeys filled with holy men, where you and Heaven are daily praised:
You, my lord, to think of dying? on my conscience I'm amazed!"

"Nay, I feel," replied King Canute, "that my end is drawing near." 40
"Don't say so," exclaimed the courtiers (striving each to squeeze a tear).
"Sure your grace is strong and lusty, and may live this fifty year."

"Live these fifty years!" the bishop roared, with actions made to suit.
"Are you mad, my good lord keeper, thus to speak of King Canute!
Men have lived a *thousand* years, and sure his majesty will do 't

"Adam, Enoch, Lamech, Cainan, Mahalaleel, Methuselah,
Lived nine hundred years apiece, and mayn't the king as well as they?"
"Fervently," exclaimed the keeper, "fervently I trust he may."

"*He* to die?" resumed the bishop. "He a mortal like to *us?*
Death was not for him intended, though *communis omnibus:* 50
Keeper, you are irreligious, for to talk and cavil thus.

"With his wondrous skill in healing ne'er a doctor can compete,
Loathsome lepers, if he touch them, start up clean upon their feet;
Surely he could raise the dead up, did his Highness think it meet.

"Did not once the Jewish captain stay the sun upon the hill,
And, the while he slew the foemen, bid the silver moon stand still?
So, no doubt, could gracious Canute, if it were his sacred will."

"Might I stay the sun above us, good Sir Bishop?" Canute cried;
"Could I bid the silver moon to pause upon her heavenly ride?
If the moon obeys my orders, sure I can command the tide. 60

"Will the advancing waves obey me, bishop, if I make the sign?"
Said the bishop, bowing lowly, "Land and sea, my lord, are thine."
Canute turned towards the ocean—"Back!" he said, "thou foaming brine!

"From the sacred shore I stand on, I command thee to retreat;
Venture not, thou stormy rebel, to approach thy master's seat:
Ocean, be thou still! I bid thee come not nearer to my feet!"

But the sullen ocean answered with a louder, deeper roar,
And the rapid waves drew nearer, falling sounding on the shore;
Back the keeper and the bishop, back the king and courtiers bore.

And he sternly bade them never more to kneel to human clay, 70
But alone to praise and worship That which earth and seas obey:
And his golden crown of empire never wore he from that day.

W. M. THACKERAY.

HE NEVER SMILED AGAIN

(1120)

The bark that held a prince went down,
  The sweeping waves rolled on;
And what was England's glorious crown
  To him that wept a son?
He lived—for life may long be borne
  Ere sorrow break its chain;—
Why comes not death to those who mourn?—
  He never smiled again!

There stood proud forms around his throne,
  The stately and the brave; 10
But which could fill the place of one,
  That one beneath the wave?
Before him passed the young and fair,
  In pleasure's reckless train;
But seas dashed o'er his son's bright hair—
  He never smiled again!

He sat where festal bowls went round,
  He heard the minstrel sing;
He saw the tourney's victor crowned
  Amidst the knightly ring; 20
A murmur of the restless deep
  Was blent with every strain,
A voice of winds that would not sleep—
  He never smiled again!

Hearts, in that time, closed o'er the trace
  Of vows once fondly poured;
And strangers took the kinsman's place
  At many a joyous board;
Graves, which true love had bathed with tears,
  Were left to Heaven's bright rain; 30
Fresh hopes were born for other years—
  He never smiled again!

MRS. HEMANS.

KING JOHN AND THE ABBOT OF CANTERBURY

An ancient story I'll tell you anon
Of a notable prince, that was called King John;
And he ruled England with main and with might,
For he did great wrong, and maintain'd little right.

And I'll tell you a story, a story so merry,
Concerning the Abbot of Canterbury;
How for his house-keeping, and high renown,
They rode post for him to London town.

An hundred men, the king did hear say,
The abbot kept in his house every day; 10
And fifty gold chains, without any doubt,
In velvet coats waited the abbot about.

"How now, father abbot, I hear it of thee,
Thou keepest a far better house than me,
And for thy house-keeping, and high renown,
I fear thou work'st treason against my crown."

"My liege," quo' the abbot, "I would it were known,
I never spend nothing but what is my own;
And I trust, your grace will do me no dere,
For spending of my own true-gotten gear." 20

"Yes, yes, father abbot, thy fault it is high,
And now for the same thou needest must die;
For except thou canst answer me questions three,
Thy head shall be smitten from thy body.

"And first," quo' the king, "when I'm in this stead,
With my crown of gold so fair on my head,
Among all my liege-men so noble of birth,
Thou must tell me to one penny what I am worth.

"Secondly, tell me, without any doubt,
How soon I may ride the whole world about; 30
And at the third question thou must not shrink,
But tell me here truly what I do think."

"O, these are hard questions for my shallow wit,
Nor I cannot answer your grace as yet;
But if you will give me but three weeks' space,
I'll do my endeavour to answer your grace."

"Now three weeks' space to thee will I give,
And that is the longest time thou hast to live;
For if thou dost not answer my questions three,
Thy lands and thy livings are forfeit to me." 40

Away rode the abbot all sad at that word,
And he rode to Cambridge, and Oxenford;
But never a doctor there was so wise,
That could with his learning an answer devise.

Then home rode the abbot of comfort so cold,
And he met his shepherd a going to fold:
"How now, my lord abbot, you are welcome home;
What news do you bring us from good king John?"

"Sad news, sad news, shepherd, I must give;
That I have but three days more to live: 50
For if I do not answer him questions three,
My head will be smitten from my body.

"The first is to tell him there in that stead,
With his crown of gold so fair on his head,
Among all his liege-men so noble of birth,
To within one penny of what he is worth.

"The second, to tell him, without any doubt,
How soon he may ride this whole world about:
And at the third question I must not shrink,
But tell him there truly what he does think." 60

"Now cheer up, sir abbot, did you never hear yet,
That a fool he may learn a wise man wit?
Lend me horse, and serving-men, and your apparel,
And I'll ride to London to answer your quarrel.

"Nay, frown not, if it hath been told unto me,
I am like your lordship as ever may be:
And if you will but lend me your gown,
There is none shall know us at fair London town."

"Now horses, and serving-men thou shalt have,
With sumptuous array most gallant and brave; 70
With crozier, and mitre, and rochet, and cope,
Fit to appear 'fore our father the Pope."

"Now welcome, sir abbot," the king he did say,
"'Tis well thou'rt come back to keep thy day;
For an if thou canst answer my questions three,
Thy life and thy living both savèd shall be.

"And first, when thou seest me here in this stead,
With my crown of gold so fair on my head,
Among all my liege-men so noble of birth,
Tell me to one penny what I am worth." 80

"For thirty pence our Saviour was sold
Among the false Jews, as I have been told;
And twenty-nine is the worth of thee,
For I think thou art one penny worser than he."

The king he laughed, and swore by St. Bittel,
"I did not think I had been worth so little!
—Now secondly tell me, without any doubt,
How soon I may ride this whole world about."

"You must rise with the sun, and ride with the same,
Until the next morning he riseth again; 90
And then your grace need not make any doubt,
But in twenty-four hours you'll ride it about."

The king he laughed, and swore by St. John,
"I did not think it could be gone so soon!
—Now from the third question thou must not shrink,
But tell me here truly what I do think."

"Yea, that I shall do, and make your grace merry:
You think I'm the abbot of Canterbury;
But I'm his poor shepherd, as plain you may see,
That am come to beg pardon for him and for me." 100

The king he laughed, and swore by the mass,
"I'll make thee lord abbot this day in his place!"
"Now nay, my liege, be not in such speed,
For alack, I can neither write, nor read."

"Four nobles a week, then, I will give thee,
For this merry jest thou hast shown unto me;
And tell the old abbot when thou comest home,
Thou hast brought him a pardon from good king
John."

Traditional Ballad.

LAMENT FOR SIMON DE MONTFORT

(Battle of Evesham, 1265)

In song my grief shall find relief,
Sad is my verse and rude;
I sing in tears our gentle peers
Who fell for England's good.
Our peace they sought, for us they fought,
For us they dared to die;
And where they sleep, a mangled heap,
Their wounds for vengeance cry.

On Evesham's plain is Montfort slain,
Well skill'd the war to guide; 10
Where streams his gore shall all deplore
Fair England's flower and pride.

Ere Tuesday's sun its course had run
  Our noblest chiefs had bled.
While rush'd to fight each gallant knight,
  Their dastard vassals fled.
Still undismay'd, with trenchant blade
  They hew'd their desperate way:
Not strength or skill to Edward's will,
  But numbers gave the day. 20

On Evesham's plain, &c.

Yet, by the blow that laid thee low,
  Brave earl, one palm was given;
Nor less at thine than Becket's shrine
  Shall rise our vows to heaven!
Our church and laws, your common cause,
  'Twas his the church to save,
Our rights restor'd, thou, generous lord,
  Shalt triumph in thy grave.

On Evesham's plain, &c. 30

Dispenser true, the good sir Hugh,
  Our justice and our friend,
Borne down with wrong, amidst the throng,
  Has met his wretched end.
Sir Henry's fate need I relate,
  Our Leicester's gallant son,
Or many a score of heroes more
  By Gloucester's hate undone?

On Evesham's plain, &c.

Each righteous lord who braved the sword, 40
  And for our safety died,
With conscience pure shall aye endure,
  Our martyr'd saint beside.

That martyr'd saint was never faint
To ease the poor man's care;
With gracious will he shall fulfil
Our just and earnest prayer.

On Evesham's plain, &c.

On Montfort's breast a hair-cloth vest
His pious soul proclaim'd; 50
With ruffian hand, the ruthless band
That sacred emblem maim'd:
And, to assuage their impious rage,
His lifeless corpse defaced,
Whose powerful arm long saved from harm
The realm his virtues graced.

On Evesham's plain, &c.

Brave martyr'd chief! no more our grief
For thee or thine shall flow;
Among the bless'd in heaven ye rest 60
From all your toils below.
But for the few, the gallant crew,
Who here in bonds remain,
Christ condescend their woes to end,
And break the tyrant's chain!

On Evesham's plain, &c.

Tr. by G. Ellis.

ROBIN HOOD AND THE THREE SQUIRES

There are twelve months in all the year,
  As I hear many men say,
But the merriest month in all the year
  Is the merry month of May.

Now Robin Hood is to Nottingham gone,
  With a link a down and a day,
And there he met a silly old woman,
  Was weeping on the way.

"What news, what news, thou silly old woman?
  What news hast thou for me?" 10
Said she, "There's three squires in Nottingham town
  To-day is condemned to die."

"O what have they done?" said Robin Hood,
  "I pray thee tell to me."
"It's for slaying of the King's fallow deer,
  Bearing their long-bows with thee."

Now Robin Hood is to Nottingham gone,
  With a link a down and a day,
And there he met with a silly old palmer,
  Was walking along the highway. 20

"What news, what news, thou silly old man?
  What news, I do thee pray."
Said he, "Three squires in Nottingham town
  Are condemned to die this day."

"Come, change thy apparel with me, old man,
  Come, change thy apparel for mine;
Here is forty shillings in good silver—
  Go drink it in beer or wine."

"O thine apparel is good," he said,
  "And mine is ragged and torn; 30
Wherever you go, wherever you ride,
  Laugh ne'er an old man to scorn."

"Come change thy apparel with me, old churl,
  Come change thy apparel with mine;
Here are twenty pieces of good broad gold,
  Go feast thy brethren with wine."

Then he put on the old man's hat,
  It stood full high on the crown:
"The first bold bargain that I come at,
  It shall make thee come down." 40

Then he put on the old man's cloak,
  Was patched black, blue, and red;
He thought no shame all the day long
  To wear the bags of bread.

Then he put on the old man's breeks,
  Was patched from side to side.
"By the truth of my body," bold Robin can say,
  "This man loved little pride."

Then he put on the old man's hose,
  Were patched from knee to wrist: 50
"By the truth of my body," said bold Robin Hood,
  "I'd laugh if I had any list."

Then he put on the old man's shoes,
  Were patched both beneath and aboon;
Then Robin Hood swore a solemn oath,
  "It's good habit that makes a man."

Now Robin Hood is to Nottingham gone,
  With a link a down and a down,
And there he met with the proud sheriff,
  Was walking along the town. 60

"O save, O save, O sheriff," he said,
  "O save, and you may see;
And what will you give to a silly old man
  To-day will your hangman be?"

"Some suits, some suits," the sheriff he said,
  "Some suits I'll give to thee;
Some suits, some suits, and pence thirteen
  To-day's a hangman's fee."

Then Robin he turns him round about,
  And jumps from stock to stone; 70
"By the truth of my body," the sheriff he said,
  "That's well jumpt, thou nimble old man."

"I was ne'er a hangman in all my life,
  Nor yet intend to trade;
But curst be he," said bold Robin,
  "That first a hangman was made.

I've a bag for meal, and a bag for malt,
  And a bag for barley and corn;
A bag for bread, and a bag for beef,
  And a bag for my little small horn. 80

"I have a horn in my pocket,
  I got it from Robin Hood;
And still when I set it to my mouth,
  For thee it blows little good."

"O wind thy horn, thou proud fellow,
  Of thee I have no doubt;
I wish that thou give such a blast
  Till both thine eyes fall out."

The first loud blast that he did blow,
  He blew both loud and shrill; 90
A hundred and fifty of Robin Hood's men
  Came riding over the hill.

The next loud blast that he did give,
  He blew both loud and amain;
And quickly sixty of Robin Hood's men
  Came shining over the plain.

"O who are you?" the sheriff he said,
  "Come tripping over the lee?"
"They're my attendants," brave Robin did say,
  "They'll pay a visit to thee." 100

They took the gallows from the slack,
  They set it in the glen;
They hang'd the proud sheriff on that,
  Released their own three men.

Traditional Ballad.

BOLD ROBIN.

Bold Robin has robed him in ghostly attire,
And forth he is gone like a holy friar,
  Singing, hey down, ho down, down, derry down:
And of two grey friars he soon was aware,
Regaling themselves with dainty fare,
  All on the fallen leaves so brown.

"Good morrow, good brothers," said bold Robin Hood,
"And what make you in good greenwood?
  Singing, hey down, ho down, down, derry down:
Now give me, I pray you, wine and food; 10
For none can I find in the good greenwood,
  All on the fallen leaves so brown."

"Good brother," they said, "we would give you full
    fain,
But we have no more than enough for twain,
  Singing, hey down, ho down, down, derry down."
"Then give me some money," said bold Robin Hood,
"For none can I find in the good greenwood,
  All on the fallen leaves so brown."

"No money have we, good brother," said they:
"Then," said he, "we three for money will pray, 20
  Singing, hey down, ho down, down, derry down:
And whatever shall come at the end of our prayer,
We three holy friars will piously share,
  All on the fallen leaves so brown."

"We will not pray with thee, good brother, God wot;
For truly, good brother, thou pleases us not,
  Singing, hey down, ho down, down, derry down."
Then up they both started from Robin to run,
But down on their knees Robin pulled them each one,
  All on the fallen leaves so brown. 30

The grey friars prayed with a doleful face,
But bold Robin prayed with a right merry grace,
  Singing, hey down, ho down, down, derry down:
And when they had prayed, their portmanteau he
    took,
And from it a hundred good angels he shook
  All on the fallen leaves so brown.

"The saints," said bold Robin, "have hearkened our
    prayer,
And here's a good angel apiece for your share;
If more you would have, you must win ere you wear,
  Singing, hey down, ho down, down, derry down." 40
Then he blew his good horn with a musical cheer,
And fifty green bowmen came trooping full near,
And away the grey friars they bounded like deer,
  All on the fallen leaves so brown.

T. L. Peacock.

DURHAM FIELD.

(1346)

Lordings, listen and hold you still;
  Hearken to me a little spell;
I shall you tell of the fairest battle
  That ever in England befell.

For as it befell in Edward the Third's days,
  In England, where he ware the crown,
Then all the chief chivalry of England
  They busked and made them boun.

They chosen all the best archers
  That in England might be found, 10
And all was to fight with the King of France,
  Within a little stound.

And when our King was over the water,
  And on the salt sea gone,
Then tidings into Scotland came
  That all England was gone.

Bows and arrows they were all forth,
  At home was not left a man
But shepherds and millers both,
  And priests with shaven crowns. 20

Then the King of Scots in a study stood,
  As he was a man of great might;
He sware he would hold his Parliament in leeve
    London,
  If he could ride there right.

Then bespake a squire, of Scotland born,
  And said "My liege, apace,
Before you come to leeve London,
  Full sore you'll rue that race.

"There been bold yeomen in merry England,
  Husbandmen stiff and strong; 30
Sharp swords they done wear,
  Bearen bows and arrows long."

The King was angry at that word;
  A long sword out he drew,
And there before his royal company
  His own squire he slew.

Hard hansel had the Scots that day,
  That wrought them woe enow,
For then durst not a Scot speak a word
  For hanging at a bough. 40

"The Earl of Anguish, where art thou?
  In my coat-armour thou shalt be,
And thou shalt lead the forward
  Thorough the English country.

"Take thee York," then said the King,
  "In stead whereas it doth stand;
I'll make thy eldest son after thee
  Heir of all Northumberland.

"The Earl of Vaughan, where be ye?
  In my coat-armour thou shalt be; 50
The high Peak and Derbyshire
  I give it thee to thy fee."

Then came in famous Douglas,
  Says "What shall my meed be?
And I'll lead the vanward, lord,
  Thorough the English country."

"Take thee Worcester," said the King,
  "Tewkesbury, Kenilworth, Burton upon Trent;
Do thou not say another day
  But I have given thee lands and rent. 60

"Sir Richard of Edinburgh, where are ye?
  A wise man in this war!
I'll give thee Bristow and the shire
  The time that we come there.

"My lord Neville, where been ye?
  You must in these wars be;
I'll give thee Shrewsbury," says the King,
  "And Coventry fair and free.

"My lord of Hamilton, where art thou?
  Thou art of my kin full nigh; 70
I'll give thee Lincoln and Lincolnshire,
  And that's enough for thee."

By then came in William Douglas,
  As breme as any boar;
He kneeled him down upon his knees,
  In his heart he sighed sore.

Says "I have served you, my lovely liege,
  These thirty winters and four,
And in the Marshes between England and Scotland,
  I have been wounded and beaten sore. 80

"For all the good service that I have done,
  What shall my meed be?
And I will lead the vanward
  Thorough the English country."

"Ask on, Douglas," said the King,
  "And granted it shall be."
"Why then, I ask little London," says Will Douglas,
  "Gotten if that it be."

The King was wrath, and rose away;
  Says "Nay, that cannot be! 90
For that I will keep for my chief chamber,
  Gotten if it be.

"But take thee North Wales and Westchester,
  The country all round about,
And rewarded thou shalt be,
  Of that take thou no doubt."

Five score knights he made on a day,
  And dubb'd them with his hands;
Rewarded them right worthily
  With the towns in merry England. 100

And when the fresh knights they were made,
  To battle they busk them boun;
James Douglas went before,
  And he thought to have won him shoon.

But they were met in a morning of May
  With the communalty of little England;
But there 'scaped never a man away,
  Through the might of Christës hand.

But all only James Douglas;
  In Durham in the field 110
An arrow struck him in the thigh;
  Fast flings he towards the King.

The King looked toward little Durham,
  Says "All things is not well!
For James Douglas bears an arrow in his thigh,
  The head of it is of steel.

"How now, James?" then said the King,
  "How now, how may this be?
And where been all thy merry men
  That thou took hence with thee?" 120

"But cease, my King," says James Douglas,
  "Alive is not left a man!"
"Now by my faith," says the King of the Scots,
  "That gate was evil gone.

"But I'll revenge thy quarrel well,
  And of that thou may be fain;
For one Scot will beat five Englishmen,
  If they meeten them on the plain."

"Now hold your tongue," says James Douglas,
  "For in faith that is not so; 130
For one Englishman is worth five Scots,
  When they meeten together tho.

"For they are as eager men to fight
  As a falcon upon a prey;
Alas! if ever they win the vanward,
  There scapes no man away."

"O peace thy talking," said the King,
"They be but English knaves,
But shepherds and millers both,
And priests with their staves." 140

The King sent forth one of his heralds of armes
To view the Englishmen.
"Be of good cheer," the herald said,
"For against one we be ten."

"Who leads those lads?" said the King of Scots,
"Thou herald, tell thou me."
The herald said "The Bishop of Durham
Is captain of that company.

"For the Bishop hath spread the King's banner,
And to battle he busks him boun." 150
"I swear by St Andrew's bones," says the King,
"I'll rap that priest on the crown."

The King looked towards little Durham,
And that he well beheld,
That the Earl Percy was well armed,
With his battle-axe entered the field.

The King looked again towards little Durham,
Four ancients there see he;
There were two standards, six in a valley,
He could not see them with his eye. 160

My lord of York was one of them,
My lord of Carlisle was the other,
And my lord Fluwilliams,
The one came with the other.

The Bishop of Durham commanded his men,
  And shortly he them bade,
That never a man should go to the field to fight
  Till he had served his God.

Five hundred priests said mass that day
  In Durham in the field, 170
And afterwards, as I heard say,
  They bare both spear and shield.

The Bishop of Durham orders himself to fight
  With his battle-axe in his hand;
He said "This day now I will fight
  As long as I can stand!"

"And so will I," said my lord of Carlisle,
  "In this fair morning gay."
"And so will I," said my lord Fluwilliams,
  "For Mary, that mild may." 180

Our English archers bent their bows
  Shortly and anon;
They shot over the Scottish host
  And scantly touched a man.

"Hold down your hands," said the Bishop of Durham,
  "My archers good and true."
The second shoot that they shot,
  Full sore the Scots it rue.

The Bishop of Durham spoke on high
  That both parties might hear. 190
"Be of good cheer, my merry men all,
  The Scots flien and changen their cheer."

But as they saiden, so they diden,
  They fell on heapes high;
Our Englishmen laid on with their bows
  As fast as they might dree.

The King of Scots in a study stood
  Amongst his company;
An arrow struck him thorough the nose,
  And thorough his armoury. 200

The King went to a marsh-side
  And light beside his steed;
He leaned him down on his sword-hilts
  To let his nose bleed.

There followed him a yeoman of merry England,
  His name was John of Copland;
"Yield thee, traitor!" says Copland then,
  "Thy life lies in my hand."

"How should I yield me," says the King,
  "And thou art no gentleman?" 210
"No, by my troth," says Copland there,
  "I am but a poor yeoman.

"What art thou better than I, sir King?
  Tell me, if that thou can!
What art thou better than I, sir King,
  Now we be but man to man?"

The King smote angrily at Copland then,
  Angrily in that stound;
And then Copland was a bold yeoman,
  And bore the King to the ground. 220

He set the King upon a palfrey,
  Himself upon a steed;
He took him by the bridle-rein,
  Towards London he 'gan him lead.

And when to London that he came,
  The King from France was new come home,
And there unto the King of Scots
  He said these words anon.

"How like you my shepherds and my millers?
  My priests with shaven crowns?" 230
"By my faith, they are the sorest fighting men
  That ever I met on the ground.

"There was never a yeoman in merry England
  But he was worth a Scottish knight."
"Ay, by my troth," said King Edward, and laugh,
  "For you fought all against the right."

But now the prince of merry England
  Worthily under his shield
Hath taken the King of France,
  At Poictiers in the field. 240

The prince did present his father with that food,
  The lovely King of France,
And forward of his journey he is gone.
  God send us all good chance!

"You are welcome, brother!" said the King of Scots,
  "For I am come hither too soon;
Christ leve that I had taken my way
  Unto the court of Rome!"

"And so would I," said the King of France,
  "When I came over the stream, 250
That I had taken my journey
  Unto Jerusalem!"

Thus ends the battle of fair Durham,
  In one morning of May,
The battle of Creçy, and the battle of Poictiers,
  All within one monthës day.

Then was wealth and welfare in merry England
  Solaces, game, and glee,
And every man loved other well,
  And the King loved good yeomanry. 260

But God that made the grass to grow
  And leaves on greenwood tree,
Now save and keep our noble King,
  And maintain good yeomanry!

Traditional Ballad.

CHEVY CHASE.

(1388)

God prosper long our noble King,
  Our lives and safeties all!
A woeful Hunting once there did
  In Chevy Chase befall.

To drive the deer, with hound and horn,
  Earl Percy took the way;
The child may rue, that is unborn,
  The hunting of that day!

The stout Earl of Northumberland
  A vow to God did make, 10
His pleasure in the Scottish woods,
  Three summer days to take;

The chiefest harts in Chevy Chase,
  To kill and bear away.
These tidings to Earl Douglas came
  In Scotland, where he lay.

Who sent Earl Percy present word,
  He would prevent his sport.
The English Earl, not fearing that,
  Did to the woods resort 20

With fifteen hundred bowmen bold,
  All chosen men of might,
Who knew full well, in time of need,
  To aim their shafts aright.

The gallant greyhounds swiftly ran,
  To chase the fallow deer.
On Monday they began to hunt,
  Ere daylight did appear;

And long before high noon they had
  A hundred fat bucks slain: 30
Then, having dined, the droviers went
  To rouse the deer again.

The hounds ran swiftly through the woods,
  The nimble deer to take,
That with their cries the hills and dales
  An echo shrill did make.

Lord Percy to the quarry went,
  To view the tender deer,
Quoth he, "Earl Douglas promised once
  This day to meet me here: 40

"But if I thought he would not come,
  No longer would I stay!"
With that a brave young gentleman
  Thus to the Earl did say:

"Lo! yonder doth Earl Douglas come,
  His men in armour bright;
Full twenty hundred Scottish spears
  All marching in our sight!

"All men of pleasant Tividale,
  Fast by the river Tweed." 50
"O, cease your sports!" Earl Percy said,
  "And take your bows with speed;

"And now with me, my countrymen,
  Your courage forth advance;
For there was never champion yet,
  In Scotland, nor in France,

"That ever did on horseback come,
  But and if my hap it were,
I durst encounter man for man,
  With him to break a spear!" 60

Earl Douglas, on his milk-white steed,
  Most like a baron bold,
Rode foremost of his company,
  Whose armour shone like gold.

"Show me," said he, "whose men ye be,
  That hunt so boldly here—
That, without my consent, do chase
  And kill my fallow deer."

The first man that did answer make,
  Was noble Percy he, 70
Who said, "We list not to declare,
  Nor show whose men we be:

"Yet we will spend our dearest blood,
  Thy chiefest harts to slay."
Then Douglas swore a solemn oath,
  And thus in rage did say:

"Ere thus I will outbravèd be,
  One of us two shall die:
I know thee well! An earl thou art;
  Lord Percy, so am I. 80

"But, trust me, Percy, pity it were,
  And great offence, to kill
Any of these, our guiltless men,
  For they have done no ill.

"Let thou and I the battle try;
  And set our men aside."
"Accursed be he," Earl Percy said,
  "By whom it is denied!"

Then stepped a gallant squire forth,
  Witherington was his name, 90
Who said, "I would not have it told
  To Henry our King, for shame,

"That e'er my Captain fought on foot,
  And I stood looking on.
You be two earls," quoth Witherington,
  "And I a squire alone.

"I'll do the best that do I may,
  While I have power to stand:
While I have power to wield my sword,
  I'll fight with heart and hand." 100

Our English archers bent their bows,
  Their hearts were good and true.
At the first flight of arrows sent,
  Full fourscore Scots they slew.

To drive the deer with hound and horn,
  Douglas bade on the bent.
Two captains moved with mickle might;
  Their spears to shivers went.

They closed full fast on every side;
  No slackness there was found: 110
But many a gallant gentleman
  Lay gasping on the ground.

O Christ! it was great grief to see,
  How each man chose his spear,
And how the blood out of their breasts
  Did gush like water clear.

At last, these two stout earls did meet,
  Like captains of great might;
Like lions wood they laid on load,
  And made a cruel fight: 120

They fought, until they both did sweat,
  With swords of tempered steel,
Till blood adown their cheeks like rain
  They trickling down did feel.

"O yield thee, Percy," Douglas said,
  "And in faith I will thee bring,
Where thou shalt high advancèd be,
  By James, our Scottish King!

"Thy ransom I will freely give,
  And this report of thee— 130
Thou art the most courageous knight
  That ever I did see!"

"No, Douglas," quoth Earl Percy then,
  "Thy proffer I do scorn;
I will not yield to any Scot
  That ever yet was born!"

With that, there came an arrow keen
  Out of an English bow,
Which struck Earl Douglas on the breast
  A deep and deadly blow; 140

Who never said more words than these,
  "Fight on, my merry men all!
Forwhy my life is at an end;
  Lord Percy sees my fall!"

Then leaving life, Earl Percy took
  The dead man by the hand,
Who said, "Earl Douglas, for thy sake,
  Would I had lost my land!

"O Christ! my very heart doth bleed
For sorrow, for thy sake, 150
For, sure, a more redoubted knight
Mischance could never take!"

A knight amongst the Scots there was,
Which saw Earl Douglas die;
Who straight in heart did vow revenge
Upon the Lord Percy.

Sir Hugh Montgomery was he called;
Who, with a spear full bright,
Well mounted on a gallant steed,
Ran fiercely through the fight, 160

And passed the English archers all,
Without all dread or fear;
And through Earl Percy's body then
He thrust his hateful spear.

With such a vehement force and might,
His body he did gore,
The staff ran through the other side,
A large cloth-yard and more.

Thus did both those nobles die,
Whose courage none could stain; 170
An English archer then perceived
The noble earl was slain.

He had a good bow in his hand,
Made of a trusty tree.
An arrow of a cloth-yard long
To the hard head haled he.

Against Sir Hugh Montgomery,
  So right the shaft he set;
The grey-goose wing that was thereon,
  In his heart's blood was wet. 180

This fight from break of day did last
  Till setting of the sun:
For when they rang the evening bell,
  The battle scarce was done.

With stout Earl Percy there was slain
  Sir John of Egerton,
Sir Robert Radcliffe, and Sir John,
  Sir James, that bold Baron.

And with Sir George and stout Sir James,
  Both knights of good account, 190
Good Sir Ralph Raby there was slain,
  Whose prowess did surmount.

For Witherington needs must I wail,
  As one in doleful dumps,
For when his legs were smitten off,
  He fought upon his stumps.

And with Earl Douglas there were slain
  Sir Hugh Montgomery;
And Sir Charles Murray, that from field
  One foot would never flee. 200

Sir Charles Murray of Ratcliffe, too,
  His sister's son was he:
Sir David Lamb, so well esteemed,
  But saved he could not be.

And the Lord Maxwell, in like case,
  Did with Earl Douglas die.
Of twenty hundred Scottish spears
  Scarce fifty-five did fly.

Of fifteen hundred Englishmen,
  Went home but fifty-three; 210
The rest in Chevy Chase were slain,
  Under the greenwood tree.

Next day did many widows come
  Their husbands to bewail:
They washed their wounds in brinish tears;
  But all would not prevail.

Their bodies, bathed in purple blood,
  They bore with them away.
They kissed them, dead, a thousand times,
  Ere they were clad in clay. 220

The news was brought to Edinborough,
  Where Scotland's king did reign,
That brave Earl Douglas suddenly
  Was with an arrow slain.

"O, heavy news!" King James did say,
  "Scotland may witness be,
I have not any captain more
  Of such account as he!"

Like tidings to King Henry came,
  Within as short a space, 230
That Percy of Northumberland,
  Was slain in Chevy Chase.

"Now, God be with him!" said our King,
"Sith it will no better be;
I trust I have, within my realm,
Five hundred as good as he.

"Yet shall not Scots, nor Scotland, say
But I will vengeance take;
And be revengèd on them all,
For brave Earl Percy's sake." 240

This vow the King did well perform
After, on Humbledown,
In one day fifty knights were slain,
With lords of great renown;

And of the rest, of small account,
Did many thousands die.
Thus endeth the hunting in Chevy Chase,
Made by the Earl Percy.

God save our King; and bless this land
With plenty, joy, and peace! 250
And grant henceforth, that foul debate
'Twixt noblemen may cease!

Traditional Ballad.

THE BATTLE OF HARLAW.

(1411)

As I cam in by Dunidier,
  An' doun by Netherha',
There was fifty thousand Hielan'men
  A-marching to Harlaw.
  Wi' a dree dree dradie drumtie dree.

As I cam on, an' farther on,
  An' doun an' by Balquhain,
Oh there I met Sir James the Rose,
  Wi' him Sir John the Gryme.

"O cam ye frae the Hielan's, man? 10
  An' cam ye a' the wey?
Saw ye Macdonell an' his men,
  As they cam frae the Skee?"

"Yes, me cam frae ta Hielan's, man,
  An' me cam a' ta wey,
An' she saw Macdonell an' his men,
  As they cam frae ta Skee."

"Oh was ye near Macdonell's men?
  Did ye their numbers see?
Come, tell to me, John Hielan'man, 20
  What micht their numbers be?"

"Yes, me was near, an' near eneuch,
  An' me their numbers saw;
There was fifty thousan' Hielan'men
  A-marchin' to Harlaw."

"Gin that be true," says James the Rose,
"We'll no come meikle speed;
We'll cry upo' our merry men,
And lichtly mount our steed."

"Oh no, oh no," says John the Gryme, 30
"That thing maun never be;
The gallant Grymes were never bate,
We'll try phat we can dee."

As I cam on, an' farther on,
An' doun an' by Harlaw,
They fell fu' close on ilka side;
Sic fun ye never saw.

They fell fu' close on ilka side,
Sic fun ye never saw;
For Hielan' swords gi'ed clash for clash, 40
At the battle o' Harlaw.

The Hielan'men, wi' their lang swords,
They laid on us fu' sair,
An' they drave back our merry men
Three acres breadth an' mair.

Brave Forbës to his brither did say,
"Noo, brither, dinna ye see?
They beat us back on ilka side,
An' we'se be forced to flee."

"Oh no, oh no, my brither dear, 50
That thing maun never be;
Tak' ye your good sword in your hand,
An' come your wa's wi' me."

"Oh no, oh no, my brither dear,
  The clans they are ower strang,
An' they drive back our merry men,
  Wi' swords baith sharp an' lang."

Brave Forbës drew his men aside,
  Said "Tak' your rest awhile,
Until I to Drumminnor send, 60
  To fess my coat o' mail."

The servant he did ride,
  An' his horse it did na fail,
For in twa hours an' a quarter
  He brocht the coat o' mail.

Then back to back the brithers twa
  Gaed in amo' the thrang,
An' they hewed down the Hielan'men,
  Wi' swords baith sharp an' lang.

Macdonell he was young an' stout, 70
  Had on his coat o' mail,
An' he has gane oot throw them a',
  To try his han' himsell.

The first ae straik that Forbës strack,
  He garrt Macdonell reel,
An' the neist ae straik that Forbës strack,
  The great Macdonell fell.

An' siccan a lierachie
  I'm sure ye never saw
As wis amo' the Hielan'men, 80
  When they saw Macdonell fa'.

An' when they saw that he was deid,
  They turn'd an' ran awa',
An' they buried him in Leggett's Den,
  A large mile frae Harlaw.

They rade, they ran, an' some did gang,
  They were o' sma' record;
But Forbës an' his merry men,
  They slew them a' the road.

On Monanday, at mornin', 90
  The battle it began,
On Saturday, at gloamin',
  Ye'd scarce kent wha had wan.

An' sic a weary buryin'
  I'm sure ye never saw
As wis the Sunday after that,
  On the muirs aneath Harlaw.

Gin ony body speer at you
  For them ye took awa',
Ye may tell their wives and bairnies 100
  They're sleepin' at Harlaw.

Traditional Ballad.

THE AGINCOURT SONG.

(1415)

Our king went forth to Normandy
With grace and might of chivalry;
There God for him wrought marvellously.
Wherefore England may call and cry
Deo gratias, Anglia,
Redde pro victoria!

He set a siege, the sooth for to say,
To Harfleur town with royal array.
That town he won, and made a fray
That France shall rue till Doomës-day. 10
Deo gratias, Anglia,
Redde pro victoria!

Then went our king, with all his host,
Through France, for all the Frenchë boast.
He spared for dread of least nor most
Till he came to Agincourt coast.
Deo gratias, Anglia,
Redde pro victoria!

Then went him forth our king comely,
In Agincourt Field he fought manly. 20
Through grace of God most marvellously
He had both field and victory.
Deo gratias, Anglia,
Redde pro victoria!

There lordës, earlës, and baroune,
Were slain and taken and that full soon,
And some were brought into London,
With joy and bliss and great renown.
Deo gratias, Anglia,
Redde pro victoria! 30

Almighty God, he keep our king,
His people, and all his well-willing,
And give them grace without ending!
Then may we call and safely sing
Deo gratias, Anglia,
Redde pro victoria!

Contemporary Poem.

KING HENRY THE FIFTH'S CONQUEST OF FRANCE.

(1415)

As our king lay musing on his bed,
He bethought himself upon a time
Of a tribute that was due from France,
Had not been paid for so long a time.

He callëd for his lovely page,
His lovely page then callëd he,
Saying, "You must go to the king of France,
To the king of France, sir, ride speedily."

O then went away this lovely page,
  This lovely page then away went he; 10
And when he came to the king of France,
  Low he fell down on his bended knee.

"My master greets you, worthy sir;
  Ten ton of gold that is due to he,
That you will send him his tribute home,
  Or in French land you soon will him see."

"Your master's young and of tender years,
  Not fit to come into my degree,
And I will send him three tennis-balls,
  That with them he may learn to play." 20

O then returned this lovely page,
  This lovely page then returned he,
And when he came to our gracious king,
  Low he fell down on his bended knee.

"What news, what news, my trusty page?
  What is the news you have brought to me?"
"I have brought such news from the king of France,
  That you and he will never agree.

"He say you're young and of tender years,
  Not fit to come into his degree, 30
And he will send you three tennis-balls,
  That with them you may learn to play."

"Recruit me Cheshire and Lancashire,
  And Derby Hills that are so free;
No married man, nor no widow's son;
  For no widow's curse shall go with me."

They recruited Cheshire and Lancashire,
  And Derby Hills that are so free;
No married man, nor no widow's son;
  Yet there was a bold jovial company. 40

O then we marched into the French land,
  With drums and trumpets so merrily;
And then bespoke the king of France,
  "Lo, yonder comes proud King Henry."

The first shot that the Frenchmen gave,
  They killed our Englishmen so free;
We killed ten thousand of the French,
  And the rest of them they ran away.

And then we marched to Paris' gates,
  With drums and trumpets so merrily; 50
O then bespoke the king of France,
  "The Lord have mercy on my men and me!

"O I will send him his tribute home,
  Ten ton of gold that is due to he,
And the finest flower that is in all France
  To the Rose of England I will give free."

Traditional Ballad.

AGINCOURT.

(1415)

Fair stood the wind for France,
When we our sails advance,
Nor now to prove our chance
    Longer will tarry;
But putting to the main,
At Caux, the mouth of Seine,
With all his martial train,
    Landed King Harry.

And taking many a fort,
Furnished in warlike sort, 10
Marched towards Agincourt
    In happy hour,
Skirmishing day by day
With those that stopped his way,
Where the French gen'ral lay
    With all his power:

Which, in his height of pride,
King Henry to deride,
His ransom to provide
    To the king sending; 20
Which he neglects the while
As from a nation vile,
Yet with an angry smile
    Their fall portending.

And turning to his men,
Quoth our brave Henry then,
"Though they to one be ten,
    Be not amazèd.
Yet have we well begun,
Battles so bravely won   30
Have ever to the sun
    By fame been raisèd.

"And for myself," quoth he,
"This my full rest shall be:
England ne'er mourn for me,
    Nor more esteem me;
Victor I will remain
Or on this earth lie slain;
Never shall she sustain
    Loss to redeem me.   40

"Poitiers and Cressy tell,
When most their pride did swell,
Under our swords they fell;
    No less our skill is
Than when our grandsire great,
Claiming the regal seat,
By many a warlike feat
    Lopped the French lilies."

The Duke of York so dread
The eager vaward led;   50
With the main Henry sped,
    Amongst his henchmen;
Excester had the rear,
A braver man not there:
O Lord, how hot they were
    On the false Frenchmen!

They now to fight are gone,
Armour on armour shone,
Drum now to drum did groan,
    To hear was wonder; 60
That with the cries they make
The very earth did shake,
Trumpet to trumpet spake,
    Thunder to thunder.

Well it thine age became,
O noble Erpingham,
Which did the signal aim
    To our hid forces!
When from a meadow by,
Like a storm suddenly, 70
The English archery
    Struck the French horses.

With Spanish yew so strong,
Arrows a cloth-yard long,
That like to serpents stung,
    Piercing the weather;
None from his fellow starts,
But playing manly parts,
And like true English hearts
    Stuck close together. 80

When down their bows they threw,
And forth their bilbos drew,
And on the French they flew,
    Not one was tardy;
Arms were from shoulders sent,
Scalps to the teeth were rent,
Down the French peasants went;
    Our men were hardy.

This while our noble king,
His broadsword brandishing, 90
Down the French host did ding
    As to o'erwhelm it,
And many a deep wound lent,
His arms with blood besprent,
And many a cruel dent
    Bruisèd his helmet.

Glo'ster, that duke so good,
Next of the royal blood,
For famous England stood,
    With his brave brother; 100
Clarence, in steel so bright,
Though but a maiden knight,
Yet in that furious fight
    Scarce such another!

Warwick in blood did wade,
Oxford the foe invade,
And cruel slaughter made,
    Still as they ran up;
Suffolk his axe did ply,
Beaumont and Willoughby 110
Bare them right doughtily,
    Ferrers and Fanhope.

Upon Saint Crispin's Day
Fought was this noble fray,
Which fame did not delay,
    To England to carry.
O, when shall Englishmen
With such acts fill a pen,
Or England breed again
    Such a King Harry? 120

MICHAEL DRAYTON.

THE ROSE OF ENGLAND.

(1485)

Throughout a garden green and gay,
  A seemly sight it was to see
How flowers did flourish fresh and gay,
  And birds do sing melodiously.

In the midst of a garden there sprang a tree,
  Which tree was of a mickle price,
And thereupon sprang the rose so red,
  The goodliest that ever sprang on rise.

This rose was fair, fresh to behold,
  Springing with many a royal lance; 10
A crowned king, with a crown of gold,
  Over England, Ireland, and of France.

Then came in a beast men call a boar,
  And he rooted this garden up and down;
By the seed of the rose he set no store,
  But afterwards it wore the crown.

He took the branches of this rose away,
  And all in sunder did them tear,
And he buried them under a clod of clay,
  Swore they should never bloom nor bear. 20

Then came in an eagle gleaming gay,
  Of all fair birds well worth the best;
He took the branch of the rose away,
  And bore it to Latham to his nest.

But now is this rose out of England exiled,
  This certain truth I will not lain;
But if it please you to sit awhile,
  I'll tell you how the rose came in again.

At Milford Haven he entered in;
  To claim his right was his delight; 30
He brought the blue boar in with him,
  To encounter with the boar so white.

Then a messenger the rose did send
  To the eagle's nest, and bid him hie:
"To my father, the old eagle, I do me commend,
  His aid and help I crave speedily."

Says, "I desire my father at my coming
  Of men and money at my need,
And also my mother of her dear blessing;
  The better then I hope to speed." 40

And when the messenger came before th' old eagle,
  He kneeled him down upon his knee,
Saith, "Well greeteth you my lord the rose,
  He hath sent you greetings here by me.

"Safe from the seas Christ hath him sent,
  Now he is entered England within."
"Let us thank God," the old eagle did say,
  "He shall be the flower of all his kin.

"Wend away, messenger, with might and main;
  It's hard to know who a man may trust; 50
I hope the rose shall flourish again,
  And have all things at his own lust."

Then Sir Rice ap Thomas draws Wales with him;
  A worthy sight it was to see,
How the Welshmen rose wholly with him,
  And shoggèd them to Shrewsbury.

At that time was baily in Shrewsbury
  One Master Mitton, in the town;
The gates were strong, he made them fast,
  And the portcullis he let down. 60

And through a garrett of the walls,
  Over Severn these words said he;
"At these gates no man enter shall;"
  But he kept him out a night and a day.

These words Mitton did Earl Richmond tell
  (I am sure the chronicles will not lie);
But when letters came from Sir William Stanley,
  Then the gates were opened presently.

Then entered this town the noble lord,
  The Earl Richmond, the rose so red; 70
The Earl of Oxford with a sword
  Would have smit off the bailiff's head.

"But hold your hand," says Earl Richmond,
  "For His love that died upon a tree!
For if we begin to head so soon,
  In England we shall bear no degree."

"What offence have I made thee," said Earl Richmond,
  "That thou kept me out of my town?"
"I know no king," said Mitton then,
  "But Richard now that wears the crown." 80

"Why, what wilt thou say," said Earl Richmond,
"When I have put King Richard down?"
"Why, then I'll be as true to you, my lord,
After the time that I am sworn."

"Were it not great pity," said Earl Richmond,
"That such a man as this should die,
Such loyal service by him done?"
(The chronicles of this will not lie.)

"Thou shalt not be harmed in any case"—
He pardonèd him presently. 90
They stayed not past a night and a day,
But towards Newport did they hie.

But at Atherstone these lords did meet;
A worthy sight it was to see
How Earl Richmond took his hat in his hand,
And said, "Cheshire and Lancashire, welcome to me!"

But now is a bird of the eagle taken;
From the white boar he cannot flee;
Therefore the old eagle makes great moan,
And prays to God most certainly. 100

"O steadfast God, verament," he did say,
"Three Persons in one God in Trinity,
Save my son, the young eagle, this day
From all false craft and treachery!"

Then the blue boar the vanward had;
He was both wary and wise of wit;
The right hand of them he took,
The sun and wind of them to get.

Then the eagle followed fast upon his prey,
With sore dints he did them smite; 110
The talbot he bit wondrous sore,
So well the unicorn did him quite.

And then came in the hart's head;
A worthy sight it was to see,
The jackets that were of white and red,
How they laid about them lustily.

But now is the fierce field foughten and ended,
And the white boar there lieth slain,
And the young eagle is preserved,
And come to his nest again. 120

But now this garden flourishes gay
With fragrant flowers comely of hue,
And gardeners it do maintain;
I hope they will prove just and true.

Our king, he is the rose so red,
That now does flourish fresh and gay;
Confound his foes, Lord, we beseech,
And love his grace both night and day!

Traditional Ballad.

SIR ANDREW BARTON.

(1511)

As it befell in midsummer-time,
  When birds sing sweetly on every tree,
Our noble king, King Henry the Eighth,
  Over the river of Thames passed he.

He was no sooner over the river,
  Down in a forest to take the air,
But eighty merchants of London city
  Came kneeling before King Henry there.

"O ye are welcome, rich merchants,
  Good sailors, welcome unto me!" 10
They swore by the rood they were sailors good,
  But rich merchants they could not be.

"To France nor Flanders dare we not pass,
  Nor Bourdeaux voyage we dare not fare,
And all for a false robber that lies on the seas,
  And robs us of our merchants-ware."

King Henry was stout, and he turned him about,
  And swore by the Lord that was mickle of might;
"I thought he had not been in the world throughout
  That durst have wrought England such unright." 20

But ever they sighed, and said, alas!
  Unto King Henry this answer again;
"He is a proud Scot that will rob us all
  If we were twenty ships and he but one."

The king looked over his left shoulder,
Amongst his lords and barons so free;
"Have I never a lord in all my realm
Will fetch yond traitor unto me?"

"Yes, that dare I!" said my lord Charles Howard,
Near to the king whereas he did stand; 30
"If that your Grace will give me leave,
Myself will be the only man."

"Thou shalt have six hundred men," saith our king,
"And choose them out of my realm so free,
Besides mariners and boys,
To guide the great ship on the sea."

"I'll go speak with Sir Andrew," says Charles, my lord Howard,
"Upon the sea, if he be there;
I will bring him and his ship to shore,
Or before my prince I will never come near." 40

The first of all my lord did call,
A noble gunner he was one;
This man was three score years and ten,
And Peter Simon was his name.

"Peter," says he, "I must sail to the sea,
To seek out an enemy; God be my speed!
Before all others I have chosen thee;
Of a hundred gunners thou'st be my head."

"My lord," says he, "if you have chosen me
Of a hundred gunners to be the head, 50
Hang me at your mainmast tree
If I miss my mark past three pence bread."

The next of all my lord he did call,
  A noble bowman he was one;
In Yorkshire was this gentleman born,
  And William Horsley was his name.

"Horsley," says he, "I must sail to the sea,
  To seek out an enemy; God be my speed!
Before all others I have chosen thee;
  Of a hundred bowmen thou'st be my head." 60

"My lord," says he, "if you have chosen me
  Of a hundred bowmen to be the head,
Hang me at your mainmast tree
  If I miss my mark past twelve pence bread."

With pikes, and guns, and bowmen bold,
  This noble Howard is gone to the sea
On the day before midsummer-even,
  And out at Thames' mouth sailed they.

They had not sailèd days three
  Upon their journey they took in hand, 70
But there they met with a noble ship,
  And stoutly made it both stay and stand.

"Thou must tell me thy name," says Charles, my lord Howard,
  "Or who thou art, or from whence thou came,
Yea, and where thy dwelling is,
  To whom and where thy ship does belong."

"My name," says he, "is Henry Hunt,
  With a pure heart and a penitent mind;
I and my ship they do belong
  Unto the New-castle that stands upon Tyne." 80

"Now thou must tell me, Harry Hunt,
  As thou hast sailed by day and by night,
Hast thou not heard of a stout robber?
  Men call him Sir Andrew Barton, knight."

But ever he sighed, and said, "Alas!
  Full well, my lord, I know that wight;
He robbed me of my merchants-ware,
  And I was his prisoner but yesternight.

"As I was sailing upon the sea,
  And Bourdeaux voyage as I did fare, 90
He clasped me to his arch-board,
  And robbed me of all my merchants-ware.

"And I am a man both poor and bare,
  And every man will have his own of me,
And I am bound towards London to fare,
  To complain to my prince Henry."

"That shall not need," says my lord Howard;
  "If thou canst let me this robber see,
For every penny he hath taken thee fro,
  Thou shalt be rewarded a shilling," quoth he. 100

"Now God forfend," says Henry Hunt,
  "My lord, you should work so far amiss:
God keep you out of that traitor's hands!
  For you not full little what a man he is.

"He is brass within, and steel without,
  And beams he bears in his top-castle strong;
His ship hath ordnance clean round about;
  Besides, my lord, he is very well manned.

"He hath a pinnace is dearly dight,
Saint Andrew's cross, that is his guide; 110
His pinnace bears nine score men and more,
Besides fifteen cannons on every side.

"If you were twenty ships, and he but one,
Either in arch-board or in hall,
He would overcome you every one,
And if his beams they do down fall."

"This is cold comfort," says my lord Howard,
"To welcome a stranger thus to the sea;
I'll bring him and his ship to shore,
Or else into Scotland he shall carry me." 120

"Then you must get a noble gunner, my lord,
That can set well with his eye,
And sink his pinnace into the sea,
And soon then overcome will he be.

"And when that you have done this,
If you chance Sir Andrew for to board,
Let no man to his top-castle go;
And I will give you a glass, my lord,

"And then you need to fear no Scot,
Whether you sail by day or by night; 130
And tomorrow, by seven of the clock,
You shall meet with Sir Andrew Barton, knight.

"I was his prisoner but yesternight,
And he hath taken me sworn," quoth he;
"I trust my Lord God will me forgive
And if that oath then broken be.

"You must lend me six pieces, my lord," quoth he,
  "Into my ship, to sail the sea,
And tomorrow, by nine of the clock,
  Your Honour again then will I see." 140

* * * * * * * * *

And the hatch-board where Sir Andrew lay
  Is hatched with gold dearly dight.
"Now by my faith," says Charles, my lord Howard,
  "Then yonder Scot is a worthy wight!

"Take in your ancients and your standards,
  Yea, that no man shall them see,
And put me forth a white willow wand,
  As merchants use to sail the sea."

But they stirred neither top nor mast,
  But Sir Andrew they passed by. 150
"What English are yonder," said Sir Andrew,
  "That can so little courtesy?

"I have been admiral over the sea
  More than these years three;
There is never an English dog, nor Portingale,
  Can pass this way without leave of me.

"But now yonder pedlers they are past,
  Which is no little grief to me;
Fetch them back," says Sir Andrew Barton,
  "They shall all hang at my mainmast tree." 160

With that the pinnace it shot off,
  That my lord Howard might it well ken;
It struck down my lord's foremast,
  And killed fourteen of my lord his men.

"Come hither, Simon," says my lord Howard,
  "Look that thy words be true thou said;
I'll hang thee at my mainmast tree
  If thou miss thy mark past twelve pence bread."

Simon was old, but his heart it was bold;
  He took down a piece, and laid it full low; 170
He put in chain yards nine,
  Besides other great shot less and moe.

With that he let his gunshot go;
  So well he settled it with his eye,
The first sight that Sir Andrew saw,
  He saw his pinnace sunk in the sea.

When he saw his pinnace sunk,
  Lord! in his heart he was not well.
"Cut my ropes, it is time to be gone;
  I'll go fetch yond pedlers back myself!" 180

When my lord Howard saw Sir Andrew loose,
  Lord! in his heart that he was fain.
"Strike on your drums, spread out your ancients;
  Sound out your trumpets, sound out amain!"

"Fight on, my men," says Sir Andrew Barton,
  "Weet, howsoever this gear will sway,
It is my lord Admiral of England
  Is come to seek me on the sea."

Simon had a son; with shot of a gun,
  Well Sir Andrew might it ken, 190
He shot it at a privy place,
  And killed sixty more of Sir Andrew's men.

Harry Hunt came in at the other side,
  And at Sir Andrew he shot then;
He drove down his foremast tree,
  And killed eighty more of Sir Andrew's men.

"I have done a good turn," says Harry Hunt,
  "Sir Andrew is not our king's friend;
He hoped to have undone me yesternight,
  But I hope I have quit him well in the end." 200

"Ever alas!" said Sir Andrew Barton,
  "What should a man either think or say?
Yonder false thief is my strongest enemy,
  Who was my prisoner but yesterday.

"Come hither to me, thou Gordon good,
  And be thou ready at my call,
And I will give thee three hundred pound,
  If thou wilt let my beams down fall."

With that he swarved the mainmast tree,
  So did he it with might and main; 210
Horsley, with a bearing arrow,
  Strake the Gordon through the brain.

And he fell into the hatches again,
  And sore of this wound that he did bleed;
Then word went through Sir Andrew's men
  That the Gordon he was dead.

"Come hither to me, James Hamilton,
  Thou art my sister's son, I have no more;
I will give thee six hundred pound
  If thou will let my beams down fall." 220

With that he swarved the mainmast tree,
  So did he it with might and main;
Horsley, with another broad arrow,
  Strake the yeoman through the brain.

That he fell down to the hatches again;
  Sore of his wound that he did bleed.
Covetousness gets no gain,
  It is very true as the Welshman said.

But when he saw his sister's son slain,
  Lord! in his heart he was not well. 230
"Go fetch me down my armour of proof,
  For I will to the top-castle myself.

"Go fetch me down my armour of proof,
  For it is gilded with gold so clear;
God be with my brother, John of Barton!
  Amongst the Portingales he did it wear."

But when he had his armour of proof,
  And on his body he had it on,
Every man that looked at him
  Said, gun nor arrow he need fear none. 240

"Come hither, Horsley," says my lord Howard,
  "And look your shaft that it go right;
Shoot a good shoot in the time of need,
  And for thy shooting thou'st be made a knight."

"I'll do my best," says Horsley then,
  "Your honour shall see before I go;
If I should be hanged at your mainmast,
  I have in my ship but arrows two."

But at Sir Andrew he shot then;
  He made sure to hit his mark; 250
Under the spole of his right arm
  He smote Sir Andrew quite through the heart.

Yet from the tree he would not start,
  But he clinged to it with might and main;
Under the collar then of his jack
  He strake Sir Andrew through the brain.

"Fight on, my men," says Sir Andrew Barton,
  "I am hurt, but I am not slain;
I'll lay me down and bleed awhile,
  And then I'll rise and fight again. 260

"Fight on, my men," says Sir Andrew Barton,
  "These English dogs they bite so low;
Fight on for Scotland and Saint Andrew
  Till you hear my whistle blow!"

But when they could not hear his whistle blow,
  Says Harry Hunt, "I'll lay my head
You may board yonder noble ship, my lord,
  For I know Sir Andrew he is dead."

With that they boarded this noble ship,
  So did they it with might and main; 270
They found eighteen score Scots alive,
  Besides the rest were maimed and slain.

My Lord Howard took a sword in his hand,
  And smote off Sir Andrew's head;
The Scots stood by did weep and mourn,
  But never a word durst speak or say.

He caused his body to be taken down,
And over the hatch-board cast into the sea,
And about his middle three hundred crowns:
"Wheresoever thou lands, it will bury thee." 280

With his head they sailed into England again,
With right good will and force and main,
And the day before New Year's Even
Into Thames' mouth they came again.

My Lord Howard wrote to King Henry's grace,
With all the news he could him bring:
"Such a New Year's gift I have brought your Grace
As never did subject to any king.

"For merchandise and manhood,
The like is not to be found; 290
The sight of these would do you good,
For you have not the like in your English ground."

But when he heard tell that they were come,
Full royally he welcomed them home;
Sir Andrew's ship was the King's New Year's gift;
A braver ship you never saw none.

Now hath our King Sir Andrew's ship,
Beset with pearls and precious stones;
Now hath England two ships of war—
Two ships of war, before but one. 300

"Who holp to this?" says King Henry,
"That I may reward him for his pain."
"Harry Hunt, and Peter Simon,
William Horsley, and I the same."

"Harry Hunt shall have his whistle and chain,
And all his jewels, whatsoever they be,
And other rich gifts that I will not name,
For his good service he hath done me.

"Horsley, right thou'st be a knight,
Lands and livings thou shalt have store; 310
Howard shall be Earl of Nottingham,
And so was never Howard before.

"Now, Peter Simon, thou art old;
I will maintain thee and thy son;
Thou shalt have five hundred pound all in gold
For the good service that thou hast done."

Then King Henry shifted his room;
In came the Queen and ladies bright;
Other errands they had none
But to see Sir Andrew Barton, knight. 320

But when they see his deadly face,
His eyes were hollow in his head;
"I would give a hundred pound," says King Henry,
"The man were alive as he is dead!

"Yet for the manful part that he hath played,
Both here and beyond the sea,
His men shall have half a crown a day
To bring them to my brother, King Jamie."

Traditional Ballad.

FLODDEN FIELD.

(1513)

King Jamie hath made a vow,
  Keep it well if he may!
That he will be at lovely London
  Upon Saint James his day.

"Upon Saint James his day at noon,
  At fair London will I be,
And all the lords in merry Scotland,
  They shall dine there with me."

Then bespake good Queen Margaret,
  The tears fell from her eye: 10
"Leave off these wars, most noble King,
  Keep your fidelity.

"The water runs swift and wondrous deep,
  From bottom unto the brim;
My brother Henry hath men good enough;
  England is hard to win."

"Away," quoth he, "with this silly fool!
  In prison fast let her lie:
For she is come of the English blood,
  And for those words she shall die." 20

With that bespake Lord Thomas Howard,
  The queen's chamberlain that day:
"If that you put Queen Margaret to death,
  Scotland shall rue it alway."

Then in a rage King James did say,
  "Away with this foolish mome!
He shall be hanged, and the other be burned,
  So soon as I come home."

At Flodden Field the Scots came in,
  Which made our English men fain; 30
At Bramstone Green this battle was seen,
  There was King Jamie slain.

Then presently the Scots did fly,
  Their cannons they left behind;
Their ensigns gay were won all away,
  Our soldiers did beat them blind.

To tell you plain, twelve thousand were slain
  That to the fight did stand,
And many prisoners took that day,
  The best in all Scotland. 40

That day made many a fatherless child,
  And many a widow poor,
And many a Scottish gay lady
  Sat weeping in her bower.

Jack with a feather was lapt all in leather,
  His boastings were all in vain;
He had such a chance, with a new morrice dance,
  He never went home again.

Traditional Ballad.

EDINBURGH AFTER FLODDEN

(1513)

I.

News of battle!—news of battle!
  Hark! 'tis ringing down the street:
And the archways and the pavement
  Bear the clang of hurrying feet.
News of battle! who hath brought it?
  News of triumph? Who should bring
Tidings from our noble army,
  Greetings from our gallant King?
All last night we watched the beacons
  Blazing on the hills afar, 10
Each one bearing, as it kindled,
  Message of the opened war.
All night long the northern streamers
  Shot across the trembling sky:
Fearful lights that never beacon
  Save when kings or heroes die.

II.

News of battle! Who hath brought it?
  All are thronging to the gate;
"Warder—warder! open quickly!
  Man—is this a time to wait?" 20
And the heavy gates are opened:
  Then a murmur long and loud,
And a cry of fear and wonder
  Bursts from out the bending crowd.

For they see in battered harness
  Only one hard-stricken man;
And his weary steed is wounded,
  And his cheek is pale and wan:
Spearless hangs a bloody banner
  In his weak and drooping hand— 30
God! can that be Randolph Murray,
  Captain of the city band?

III.

Round him crush the people, crying,
  "Tell us all—oh, tell us true!
Where are they who went to battle,
  Randolph Murray, sworn to you?
Where are they, our brothers—children?
  Have they met the English foe?
Why art thou alone, unfollowed?
  Is it weal or is it woe?" 40
Like a corpse the grisly warrior
  Looks from out his helm of steel;
But no word he speaks in answer—
  Only with his armèd heel
Chides his weary steed, and onward
  Up the city streets they ride;
Fathers, sisters, mothers, children,
  Shrieking, praying by his side.
"By the God that made thee, Randolph!
  Tell us what mischance hath come." 50
Then he lifts his riven banner,
  And the asker's voice is dumb.

IV.

The elders of the city
  Have met within their hall—
The men whom good King James had charged
  To watch the tower and wall.
"Your hands are weak with age," he said,
  "Your hearts are stout and true;
So bide ye in the Maiden Town,
  While others fight for you. 60
My trumpet from the Border-side
  Shall send a blast so clear,
That all who wait within the gate
  That stirring sound may hear.
Or, if it be the will of Heaven
  That back I never come,
And if, instead of Scottish shouts,
  Ye hear the English drum,—
Then let the warning bells ring out,
  Then gird you to the fray, 70
Then man the walls like burghers stout,
  And fight while fight you may.
'Twere better that in fiery flame
  The roofs should thunder down,
Than that the foot of foreign foe
  Should trample in the town!"

V.

Then in came Randolph Murray,—
  His step was slow and weak
And, as he doffed his dinted helm,
  The tears ran down his cheek; 80

They fell upon his corslet
  And on his mailèd hand,
As he gazed around him wistfully,
  Leaning sorely on his brand.
And none who then beheld him
  But straight were smote with fear,
For a bolder and a sterner man
  Had never couched a spear.
They knew so sad a messenger
  Some ghastly news must bring; 90
And all of them were fathers,
  And their sons were with the King.

VI.

And up then rose the Provost—
  A brave old man was he,
Of ancient name, and knightly fame,
  And chivalrous degree.
He ruled our city like a Lord
  Who brooked no equal here,
And ever for the townsman's rights
  Stood up 'gainst prince and peer. 100
And he had seen the Scottish host
  March from the Borough-muir,
With music-storm and clamorous shout,
And all the din that thunders out
  When youth 's of victory sure.
But yet a dearer thought had he,—
  For, with a father's pride,
He saw his last remaining son
  Go forth by Randolph's side,

With casque on head and spur on heel, 110
  All keen to do and dare;
And proudly did that gallant boy
  Dunedin's banner bear.
Oh! woeful now was the old man's look,
  And he spake right heavily—
"Now, Randolph, tell thy tidings,
  However sharp they be!
Woe is written on thy visage,
  Death is looking from thy face:
Speak! though it be of overthrow— 120
  It cannot be disgrace!"

VII.

Right bitter was the agony
  That wrung that soldier proud:
Thrice did he strive to answer,
  And thrice he groaned aloud.
Then he gave the riven banner
  To the old man's shaking hand,
Saying—"That is all I bring ye
  From the bravest of the land!
Ay! ye may look upon it— 130
  It was guarded well and long,
By your brothers and your children,
  By the valiant and the strong.
One by one they fell around it,
  As the archers laid them low,
Grimly dying, still unconquered,
  With their faces to the foe.

Ay! ye may well look upon it—
  There is more than honour there,
Else, be sure, I had not brought it 140
  From the field of dark despair.
Never yet was royal banner
  Steeped in such a costly dye;
It hath lain upon a bosom
  Where no other shroud shall lie.
Sirs! I charge you, keep it holy;
  Keep it as a sacred thing,
For the stain ye see upon it
  Was the life-blood of your King!"

VIII.

Woe, and woe, and lamentation! 150
  What a piteous cry was there!
Widows, maidens, mothers, children,
  Shrieking, sobbing in despair!
Through the streets the death-word rushes,
  Spreading terror, sweeping on—
"Jesu Christ! our King has fallen—
  O Great God, King James is gone!
Holy Mother Mary, shield us,
  Thou who erst didst lose thy Son!
O the blackest day for Scotland 160
  That she ever knew before!
O our King—the good, the noble,
  Shall we see him never more?
Woe to us, and woe to Scotland!
  O our sons, our sons and men!
Surely some have 'scaped the Southron,
  Surely some will come again!"

Till the oak that fell last winter
  Shall uprear its shattered stem—
Wives and mothers of Dunedin— 170
  Ye may look in vain for them!

IX.

But within the Council Chamber
  All was silent as the grave,
Whilst the tempest of their sorrow
  Shook the bosoms of the brave.
Well indeed might they be shaken
  With the weight of such a blow:
He was gone—their prince, their idol,
  Whom they loved and worshipped so!
Like a knell of death and judgement 180
  Rung from heaven by angel hand,
Fell the words of desolation
  On the elders of the land.
Hoary heads were bowed and trembling,
  Withered hands were clasped and wrung;
God had left the old and feeble,
  He had ta'en away the young.

X.

Then the Provost he uprose,
  And his lip was ashen white;
But a flush was on his brow, 190
  And his eye was full of light.
"Thou hast spoken, Randolph Murray,
  Like a soldier stout and true;
Thou hast done a deed of daring
  Had been perilled but by few.

For thou hast not shamed to face us,
  Nor to speak thy ghastly tale,
Standing—thou a knight and captain—
  Here, alive within thy mail!
Now, as my God shall judge me, 200
  I hold it braver done,
Than hadst thou tarried in thy place,
  And died above my son!
Thou needst not tell it: he is dead.
  God help us all this day!
But speak—how fought the citizens
  Within the furious fray?
For by the might of Mary,
  'Twere something still to tell
That no Scottish foot went backward 210
  When the Royal Lion fell!"

XI.

"No one failed him. He is keeping
  Royal state and semblance still;
Knight and noble lie around him,
  Cold on Flodden's fatal hill.
Of the brave and gallant-hearted,
  Whom you sent with prayers away,
Not a single man departed
  From his Monarch yesterday.
Had you seen them, O my masters! 220
  When the night began to fall,
And the English spearmen gathered
  Round a grim and ghastly wall!

As the wolves in winter circle
  Round the leaguer on the heath,
So the greedy foe glared upward,
  Panting still for blood and death.
But a rampart rose before them,
  Which the boldest dared not scale;
Every stone a Scottish body, 230
  Every step a corpse in mail!
And behind it lay our Monarch,
  Clenching still his shivered sword;
By his side Montrose and Athole,
  At his feet a Southron lord.
All so thick they lay together,
  When the stars lit up the sky,
That I knew not who were stricken,
  Or who yet remained to die.
Few there were when Surrey halted, 240
  And his wearied host withdrew;
None but dying men around me,
  When the English trumpet blew.
Then I stooped, and took the banner,
  As you see it, from his breast,
And I closed our hero's eyelids,
  And I left him to his rest.
In the mountains growled the thunder,
  As I leaped the woeful wall,
And the heavy clouds were settling 250
  Over Flodden, like a pall."

XII.

So he ended. And the others
  Cared not any answer then;
Sitting silent, dumb with sorrow,
  Sitting anguish-struck, like men
Who have seen the roaring torrent
  Sweep their happy homes away,
And yet linger by the margin,
  Staring wildly on the spray.
But, without, the maddening tumult 260
  Waxes ever more and more,
And the crowd of wailing women
  Gather round the Council door.
Every dusky spire is ringing
  With a dull and hollow knell,
And the *Miserere's* singing
  To the tolling of the bell.
Through the streets the burghers hurry,
  Spreading terror as they go;
And the rampart's thronged with watchers 270
  For the coming of the foe.
From each mountain-top a pillar
  Streams into the torpid air,
Bearing token from the Border
  That the English host is there.
All without is flight and terror,
  All within is woe and fear—
God protect thee, Maiden City,
  For thy latest hour is near!

XIII.

No! not yet, thou high Dunedin! 280
  Shalt thou totter to thy fall;
Though thy bravest and thy strongest
  Are not there to man the wall.
No, not yet! the ancient spirit
  Of our fathers hath not gone;
Take it to thee as a buckler
  Better far than steel or stone.
Oh, remember those who perished
  For thy birthright at the time
When to be a Scot was treason, 290
  And to side with Wallace crime!
Have they not a voice among us,
  Whilst their hallowed dust is here?
Hear ye not a summons sounding
  From each buried warrior's bier?
Up!—they say—and keep the freedom
  Which we won you long ago:
Up! and keep our graves unsullied
  From the insults of the foe!
Up! and if ye cannot save them, 300
  Come to us in blood and fire:
Midst the crash of falling turrets
  Let the last of Scots expire!

XIV.

Still the bells are tolling fiercely,
  And the cry comes louder in;
Mothers wailing for their children,
  Sisters for their slaughtered kin.

All is terror and disorder;
  Till the Provost rises up,
Calm, as though he had not tasted 310
  Of the fell and bitter cup.
All so stately from his sorrow,
  Rose the old undaunted chief,
That you had not deemed, to see him,
  His was more than common grief.
"Rouse ye, Sirs!" he said; "we may not
  Longer mourn for what is done;
If our King be taken from us,
  We are left to guard his son.
We have sworn to keep the city 320
  From the foe, whate'er they be,
And the oath that we have taken
  Never shall be broke by me.
Death is nearer to us, brethren,
  Than it seemed to those who died,
Fighting yesterday at Flodden,
  By their lord and master's side.
Let us meet it then in patience,
  Not in terror or in fear;
Though our hearts are bleeding yonder, 330
  Let our souls be steadfast here.
Up, and rouse ye! Time is fleeting,
  And we yet have much to do;
Up! and haste ye through the city,
  Stir the burghers stout and true!
Gather all our scattered people,
  Fling the banner out once more,—
Randolph Murray! do thou bear it,
  As it erst was borne before:
Never Scottish heart will leave it, 340
  When they see their Monarch's gore!

XV.

"Let them cease that dismal knelling!
It is time enough to ring,
When the fortress-strength of Scotland
Stoops to ruin like its King.
Let the bells be kept for warning,
Not for terror or alarm;
When they next are heard to thunder,
Let each man and stripling arm.
Bid the women leave their wailing— 350
Do they think that woeful strain,
From the bloody heaps of Flodden,
Can redeem their dearest slain?
Bid them cease,—or rather hasten
To the churches every one;
There to pray to Mary Mother,
And to her anointed Son,
That the thunderbolt above us
May not fall in ruin yet;
That in fire and blood and rapine 360
Scotland's glory may not set.
Let them pray,—for never women
Stood in need of such a prayer!—
England's yeomen shall not find them
Clinging to the altars there.
No! if we are doomed to perish,
Man and maiden, let us fall,
And a common gulf of ruin
Open wide to whelm us all!
Never shall the ruthless spoiler 370
Lay his hot insulting hand
On the sisters of our heroes,
Whilst we bear a torch or brand!

Up! and rouse ye, then, my brothers,—
  But when next ye hear the bell
Sounding forth the sullen summons
  That may be our funeral knell,
Once more let us meet together,
  Once more see each other's face;
Then, like men that need not tremble, 380
  Go to our appointed place.
God, our Father, will not fail us,
  In that last tremendous hour,—
If all other bulwarks crumble,
  HE will be our strength and tower:
Though the ramparts rock beneath us,
  And the walls go crashing down,
Though the roar of conflagration
  Bellow o'er the sinking town;
There is yet one place of shelter, 390
  Where the foemen cannot come,
Where the summons never sounded
  Of the trumpet or the drum.
There again we'll meet our children,
  Who, on Flodden's trampled sod,
For their King and for their country
  Rendered up their souls to God.
There shall we find rest and refuge
  With our dear departed brave;
And the ashes of the city 400
  Be our universal grave!"

W. E. AYTOUN.

DICK O' THE COW.

(c. 1530)

Now Liddesdale has long lain in,
  There is no riding there at a';
Their horse is growing so lidder and fat
  That are lazy in the sta'.

Then Johnnie Armstrong to Willie can say,
  "Billie, a riding then will we;
England and us has been long at a feed;
  Perhaps we may hit of some bootie."

Then they're comed on to Hutton Hall,
  They rade that proper place about; 10
But the laird he was the wiser man,
  For he had left nae gear without.

Then he had left nae gear to steal,
  Except six sheep upon a lea;
Says Johnnie, "I'd rather in England die,
  Before their six sheep gaed to Liddesdale with me.

"But how call'd they the man we last with met,
  Billie, as we came over the know?"
"That same he is an innocent fool,
  And some men calls him Dick o' the Cow." 20

"That fool has three as good kine of his own
  As is in a' Cumberland, billie," quoth he;
"Betide my life, betide my death,
  These three kine shall go to Liddesdale with me."

Then they're comed on to the poor fool's house,
 And they have broken his walls so wide;
They have loosed out Dick o' the Cow's kine three,
 And ta'en three co'erlets off his wife's bed.

Then on the morn, when the day grew light,
 The shouts and cries rose loud and high; 30
"Hold thy tongue, my wife," he says,
 "And of thy crying let me be.

"Hold thy tongue, my wife," he says,
 "And of thy crying let me be,
And ay that where thou wants a cow,
 Good sooth that I shall bring thee three."

Then Dick's comed on to lord and master,
 And I wat a dreary fool was he;
"Hold thy tongue, my fool," he says,
 "For I may not stand to jest with thee." 40

"Shame speed a' your jesting, my lord," quo' Dickie,
 "For nae such jesting 'grees with me;
Liddesdale has been in my house this last night,
 And they have ta'en my three kine from me."

"But I may nae langer in Cumberland dwell,
 To be your poor fool and your leal,
Unless ye give me leave, my lord,
 To go to Liddesdale and steal."

"To give thee leave, my fool," he says,
 "Thou speaks against mine honour and me; 50
Unless thou give me thy troth and thy right hand,
 Thou'll steal frae nane but them that sta' from thee."

"There is my troth and my right hand;
My head shall hing on Hairibee,
I'll never cross Carlisle sands again,
If I steal frae a man but them that sta' frae me."

Dickie has ta'en leave at lord and master,
And I wot a merry fool was he;
He has bought a bridle and a pair of new spurs,
And has packed them up in his breek-thigh. 60

Then Dickie's come on for Puddinburn,
Even as fast as he may dree;
Dickie's come on for Puddinburn,
Where there was thirty Armstrongs and three.

"What's this comed on me!" quo' Dickie,
"What mickle wae's this happen'd on me," quo' he,
"Where here is but an innocent fool,
And there is thirty Armstrongs and three!"

Yet he's comed up to the hall among them all;
So well he became his courtesie; 70
"Well may ye be, my good Laird's Jock,
But the deil bless all your companie!

"I'm come to plain of your man Fair Johnnie Armstrong,
And syne his billie Willie," quo' he;
"How they have been in my house this last night,
And they have ta'en my three ky frae me."

Quo' Johnnie Armstrong, "We'll him hang;"
"Nay," then quo' Willie, "we'll him slae;"
But up bespake another young man,
"We'll knit him in a four-nooked sheet, 80
Give him his burden of batts, and let him gae."

Then up bespake the good Laird's Jock,
  The best fella in the companie;
"Sit thy way down a little while, Dickie,
  And a piece of thine own cow's hough I'll give
    to thee."

But Dickie's heart it grew so great
  That never a bit of it he dought to eat;
But Dickie was ware of an auld peat-house,
  Where there all the night he thought for to sleep.

Then Dickie was ware of that auld peat-house, 90
  Where there all the night he thought for to lie;
And a' the prayers the poor fool pray'd was,
  "I wish I had a mense for my own three ky!"

Then it was the use of Puddinburn,
  And the house of Mangertoun, all hail!
These that came not at the first call
  They got no more meat till the next meal.

The lads, that hungry and aevery was,
  Above the door-head they flang the key.
Dickie took good notice to that; 100
  Says, "There's a booty yonder for me."

Then Dickie 's gone into the stable,
  Where there stood thirty horse and three;
He has tied them a' with St. Mary knot,
  All these horse but barely three.

He has tied them a' with St. Mary knot,
  All these horse but barely three;
He has loupen on one, taken another in his hand,
  And out at the door and gone is Dickie.

Then on the morn, when the day grew light, 110
The shouts and cries rose loud and high;
"What's that thief?" quo' the good Laird's Jock,
"Tell me the truth and the verity.

"What's that thief?" quo' the good Laird's Jock,
"See unto me ye do not lie."
"Dick o' the Cow has been in the stable this last nicht,
And has my brother's horse and mine frae me."

"Ye wad never be tell'd it," quo' the Laird's Jock,
"Have ye not found my tales fu' leal?
Ye wad never out of England bide, 120
Till crooked and blind and a' wad steal."

"But will thou lend me thy bay?" Fair Johnnie Armstrong can say,
"There's nae mae horse loose in the stable but he;
And I'll either bring ye Dick o' the Cow again,
Or the day is come that he must die."

"To lend thee my bay," the Laird's Jock can say,
"He's both worth gold and good monie;
Dick o' the Cow has away twa horse,
I wish no thou should make him three."

He has ta'en the Laird's jack on his back, 130
The twa-handed sword that hang leugh by his thigh;
He has ta'en the steel cap on his head,
And on is he to follow Dickie.

Then Dickie was not a mile off the town,
I wot a mile but barely three,
Till John Armstrong has o'erta'en Dick o' the Cow,
Hand for hand on Cannobie lee.

"Abide thee, bide now, Dickie, than,
  The day is come that thou must die."
Dickie looked o'er his left shoulder, 140
  "Johnnie, has thou any mo in thy companie?

"There is a preacher in our chapel,
  And a' the lee-lang day teaches he;
When day is gone, and night is come,
  There 's never a word I mark but three.

"The first and second 's Faith and Conscience,
  The third is, Johnnie, Take heed of thee!
But what faith and conscience had thou, traitor,
  When thou took my three ky frae me?

"And when thou had ta'en my three ky, 150
  Thou thought in thy heart thou was no well sped;
But thou sent thy billie Willie o'er the know,
  And he took three co'erlets off my wife's bed."

Then Johnnie let a spear fa' leugh by his thigh,
  Thought well to run the innocent through,
But the powers above was more than his,
  He ran but the poor fool's jerkin through.

Together they ran or ever they blan;
  This was Dickie the fool, and he;
Dickie could not win to him with the blade of the
    sword, 160
  But he fell'd him with the plummet under the eye.

Now Dickie has fell'd Fair Johnnie Armstrong,
  The prettiest man in the south countrie;
"Gramercie," then can Dickie say,
  "I had twa horse, thou has made me three."

He has ta'en the laird's jack off his back,
The twa-handed sword that hang leugh by his thigh;
He has ta'en the steel cap off his head;
"Johnnie, I'll tell my master I met with thee."

When Johnnie waken'd out of his dream, 170
I wot a dreary man was he;
"Is thou gone now, Dickie, than?
The shame gae in thy companie!

"Is thou gone now, Dickie, than?
The shame go in thy companie!
For if I should live this hundred year,
I shall never fight with a fool after thee."

Then Dickie comed home to lord and master,
Even as fast as he may dree.
"Now, Dickie, I shall neither eat meat nor drink 180
Till high hanged that thou shall be!"

"The shame speed the liars, my lord!" quo' Dickie,
"That was no the promise ye made to me;
For I'd never gone to Liddesdale to steal
Till that I sought my leave at thee."

"But what gart thou steal the Laird's Jock's horse?
And, limmer, what gart thou steal him?" quo' he;
"For lang might thou in Cumberland dwelt
Or the Laird's Jock had stoln aught frae thee."

"Indeed I wot ye lied, my lord, 190
And even so loud as I hear ye lie;
I won him frae his man, Fair Johnnie Armstrong,
Hand for hand on Cannobie lee.

"There 's the jack was on his back,
The twa-handed sword that hung leugh by his thigh;
There 's the steel cap was on his head;
I have a' these tokens to let you see."

"If that be true thou to me tells
(I trow thou dare not tell a lie),
I'll give thee twenty pound for the good horse, 200
Well tell'd in thy cloak-lap shall be.

"And I'll give thee one of my best milk-ky
To maintain thy wife and children three;
And that may be as good, I think,
As ony twa o' thine might be."

"The shame speed the liars, my lord!" quo' Dickie;
"Trow ye ay to make a fool of me?
I'll either have thirty pound for the good horse,
Or else he 's gae to Mattan Fair wi' me."

Then he has given him thirty pound for the good horse, 210
All in gold and good monie:
He has given him one of his best milk-ky
To maintain his wife and children three.

Then Dickie 's come down through Carlisle town,
Even as fast as he may dree.
The first of men that he with met
Was my lord's brother, Bailiff Glazenberrie.

"Well may ye be, my good Ralph Scrupe!"
"Welcome, my brother's fool!" quo' he;
"Where did thou get Fair Johnnie Armstrong's horse?" 220
"Where did I get him but steal him," quo' he.

"But will thou sell me Fair Johnnie Armstrong's
horse?
And, billie, will thou sell him to me?" quo' he;
"Ay, and thou tell me the monie on my cloak-lap,
For there's not one farthing I'll trust thee."

"I'll give thee fifteen pound for the good horse,
Well told on thy cloak-lap shall be;
And I'll give thee one of my best milk-ky
To maintain thy wife and thy children three."

"The shame speed the liars, my lord!" quo' Dickie, 230
"Trow ye ay to make a fool of me?" quo' he;
"I'll either have thirty pound for the good horse,
Or else he's to Mattan Fair with me."

He has given him thirty pound for the good horse,
All in gold and good monie;
He has given him one of his best milk-ky
To maintain his wife and children three.

Then Dickie lap a loup on high,
And I wot a loud laughter leugh he;
"I wish the neck of the third horse were broken, 240
For I have a better of my own, and onie better
can be."

Then Dickie comed hame to his wife again.
Judge ye how the poor fool he sped!
He has given her three score of English pounds
For the three auld co'erlets was ta'en off her bed.

"Ha'e, take thee there twa as good ky,
I trow, as all thy three might be;
And yet here is a white-footed nag,
I think he'll carry both thee and me.

"But I may no longer in Cumberland dwell; 250
The Armstrongs they'll hang me high."
But Dickie has ta'en leave at lord and master,
And Burgh under Stanemuir there dwells Dickie.

EARL BOTHWELL.

(1568)

Woe worth thee, woe worth thee, false Scotland!
For thou hast ever wrought by a sleight;
For the worthiest prince that ever was born
You hanged under a cloud by night.

The Queen of France a letter wrote,
And sealed it with heart and ring,
And bade him come Scotland within,
And she would marry him and crown him king.

To be a king, it is a pleasant thing,
To be a prince unto a peer; 10
But you have heard, and so have I too,
A man may well buy gold too dear.

There was an Italian in that place
Was as well beloved as ever was he;
Lord David was his name,
Chamberlain unto the queen was he.

For if the king had risen forth of his place,
He would have sit him down in the chair,
And tho' it beseemed him not so well,
Altho' the king had been present there. 20

Some lords in Scotland waxed wondrous wroth,
  And quarrell'd with him for the nonce;
I shall you tell how it befell;
  Twelve daggers were in him all at once.

Then some of the lords of Scotland waxed wroth,
  And made their vow vehemently;
"For death of the queen's chamberlain
  The king himself he shall die."

They strowed his chamber over with gunpowder,
  And laid green rushes in his way; 30
For the traitors thought that night
  The worthy king for to betray.

To bed the worthy king made him boun;
  To take his rest, that was his desire;
He was no sooner cast on sleep
  But his chamber was on a blazing fire.

Up he lope, and a glass window broke,
  He had thirty foot for to fall;
Lord Bothwell kept a privy watch
  Underneath his castle wall. 40
"Who have we here?" said Lord Bothwell;
  "Answer me, now I do call."

"King Henry the Eighth my uncle was;
  Some pity show for his sweet sake!
Ah, Lord Bothwell, I know thee well;
  Some pity on me I pray thee take!"

"I'll pity thee as much," he said,
  "And as much favour I'll show to thee,
As thou had on the queen's chamberlain
  That day thou deemedst him to die." 50

Through halls and towers this king they led,
  Through castles and towers that were high,
Through an arbour into an orchard,
  And there hanged him in a pear tree.

When the governor of Scotland he heard tell
  That the worthy king he was slain,
He hath banished the queen so bitterly
  That in Scotland she dare not remain.

But she is fled into merry England,
  And Scotland too aside hath lain, 60
And through the Queen of England's good grace
  Now in England she doth remain.

Traditional Ballad.

THE RISING IN THE NORTH.

(1569)

Listen, lively lordings all,
  Lithe and listen unto me,
And I will sing of a noble earl,
  The noblest earl in the North Countrie.

Earl Percy is into his garden gone,
  And after him walks his fair ladie.
"I hear a bird sing in my ear
  That I must either fight or flee."

"Now heaven forefend, my dearest lord,
  That ever such harm should hap to thee, 10
But go to London to the Court;
  And fair fall truth and honesty!"

"Now nay, now nay, my lady gay,
  Alas! thy counsel suits not me;
Mine enemies prevail so fast
  That at the Court I may not be."

"O go to the Court yet, good my lord,
  And take thy gallant men with thee,
And if any dare to do you wrong
  Then your warrant they may be." 20

"Now nay, now nay, thou lady fair,
  The Court is full of subtiltie,
And if I go to the Court, lady,
  Never more I may thee see."

"Yet go to the Court, my lord," she says,
  "And I myself will go wi' thee;
At Court then for my dearest lord
  His faithful borrow I will be."

"Now nay, now nay, my lady dear,
  Far lever had I lose my life 30
Than leave among my cruel foes
  My love in jeopardy and strife.

"But come thou hither, my little foot-page,
  Come thou hither unto me,
To Maister Norton thou must go
  In all the haste that ever may be.

"Commend me to that gentleman,
  And bear this letter here fro me,
And say that earnestly I pray
  He will ride in my company." 40

One while the little foot-page went,
And another while he ran,
Until he came to his journey's end,
The little foot-page never blan.

When to that gentleman he came,
Down he kneelèd on his knee;
Quoth he, "My lord commendeth him,
And sends this letter unto thee."

And when the letter it was read
Afore that goodly company, 50
I wis if you the truth would know,
There was many a weeping eye.

He said, "Come hither, Christopher Norton,
A gallant youth thou seem'st to be,
What dost thou counsel me, my son,
Now that good earl's in jeopardy?"

"Father, my counsel's fair and free,
That earl he is a noble lord,
And whatsoever to him you hight,
I would not have you break your word." 60

"Gramercy, Christopher, my son,
Thy counsel well it liketh me,
And if we speed and 'scape with life
Well advancèd shalt thou be.

"Come you hither, my nine good sons,
Gallant men I trow you be,
How many of you, my children dear,
Will stand by that good earl and me?"

Eight of them did answer make,
  Eight of them spake hastilie: 70
"O father, till the day we die,
  We'll stand by that good earl and thee!"

"Gramercy now, my children dear,
  You show yourselves right bold and brave,
And whethersoe'er I live or die,
  A father's blessing you shall have.

"But what say'st thou, O Francis Norton?
  Thou art mine eldest son and heir;
Somewhat lies brooding in thy breast:
  Whatever it be, to me declare." 80

"Father, you are an agèd man,
  Your head is white, your beard is gray;
It were a shame at these your years,
  For you to rise in such a fray."

"Now fie upon thee, coward Francis,
  Thou never learnedst this of me;
When thou wert young and tender of age,
  Why did I make so much of thee?"

"But, father, I will wend with you,
  Unarmed and naked will I be, 90
And he that strikes against the crown,
  Ever an ill death may he dee."

Then rose that reverend gentleman,
  And with him came a goodly band
To join the brave Earl Percy,
  And all the flower o' Northumberland.

With them the noble Neville came,
  The earl of Westmoreland was he;
At Wetherby they mustered their host,
  Thirteen thousand fair to see. 100

Lord Westmoreland his ancient raised,
  The Dun Bull he raised on high;
Three Dogs with golden collars
  Were there set out most royally.

Earl Percy there his ancient spread,
  The Half-Moon shining all so fair;
The Norton's ancient had the Cross,
  And the Five Wounds our Lord did bear.

Then Sir George Bowes he straightway rose,
  After them some spoil to make; 110
Those noble earls turned back again,
  And aye they vowed that knight to take.

The baron he to his castle fled,
  To Barnard Castle then fled he;
The uttermost walls were easy to win;
  The earls have won them presently.

The uttermost walls were lime and brick,
  But though they won them soon anon,
Long ere they won the innermost walls,
  For they were cut in rock of stone. 120

Then news unto leeve London came
  In all the speed that ever may be,
And word is brought to our royal queen
  Of the rising in the North Countrie.

Her grace she turned her round about,
  And like a royal queen she swore,
"I will ordain them such a breakfast
  As never was in the North before."

She caused thirty thousand men be raised,
  With horse and harness fair to see, 130
She caused thirty thousand men be raised
  To take the earls i' th' North Countrie.

Wi' them the false Earl Warwick went,
  Th' Earl Sussex and the Lord Hunsden;
Until they to York Castle came,
  I wis they never stint ne blan.

Now spread thy ancient, Westmoreland,
  Thy Dun Bull fain would we spy,
And thou, the Earl o' Northumberland,
  Now raise thy half-moon up on high! 140

But the Dun Bull is fled and gone,
  And the Half-Moon vanished away;
The earls, though they were brave and bold,
  Against so many could not stay.

Thee, Norton, wi' thine eight good sons,
  They doom'd to die, alas! for ruth!
Thy reverend locks thee could not save,
  Nor them their fair and blooming youth.

Wi' them full many a gallant wight
  They cruelly bereaved of life, 150
And many a child made fatherless,
  And widowed many a tender wife.

Traditional Ballad.

MARY AMBREE.

(1584)

When captains courageous, whom death could not
daunt,
Did march to the siege of the city of Gaunt,
They mustered their soldiers by two and by three,
And the foremost in battle was Mary Ambree.

When brave Sir John Major was slain in her sight,
Who was her true lover, her joy, and delight,
Because he was slain most treacherouslie,
Then vowed to revenge him Mary Ambree.

She clothèd herself from the top to the toe
In buff of the bravest, most seemly to show; 10
A fair shirt of mail then slippèd on she;
Was not this a brave bonny lass, Mary Ambree?

A helmet of proof she straight did provide,
A strong arming sword she girt by her side,
On her hand a goodly fair gauntlet put she;
Was not this a brave bonny lass, Mary Ambree?

Then took she her sword and her target in hand,
Bidding all such, as would, be of her band;
To wait on her person came thousand and three;
Was not this a brave bonny lass, Mary Ambree? 20

"My soldiers," she saith, "so valiant and bold,
Now follow your captain, whom you do behold;
Still foremost in battle myself will I be."
Was not this a brave bonny lass, Mary Ambree?

Then cried out her soldiers, and loud they did say,
"So well thou becomest this gallant array,
Thy heart and thy weapons so well do agree,
There was none ever like Mary Ambree."

She cheerèd her soldiers, that foughten for life,
With ancient and standard, with drum and with
fife, 30
With brave clanging trumpets, that sounded so free;
Was not this a brave bonny lass, Mary Ambree?

"Before I will see the worst of you all
To come into danger of death, or of thrall,
This hand and this life I will venture so free."
Was not this a brave bonny lass, Mary Ambree?

She led up her soldiers in battle array,
'Gainst three times their number by break of the day;
Seven hours in skirmish continuèd she;
Was not this a brave bonny lass, Mary Ambree? 40

She fillèd the skies with the smoke of her shot,
And her enemies' bodies with bullets so hot;
For one of her own men a score killèd she;
Was not this a brave bonny lass, Mary Ambree?

And when her false gunner, to spoil her intent,
Away all her pellets and powder had sent,
Straight with her keen weapon she slashed him in
three;
Was not this a brave bonny lass, Mary Ambree?

Being falsely betrayèd for lucre of hire,
At length she was forcèd to make a retire; 50
Then her soldiers into a strong castle drew she;
Was not this a brave bonny lass, Mary Ambree?

Her foes they beset her on every side,
As thinking close siege she could never abide;
To beat down the walls they all did decree:
But stoutly defied them brave Mary Ambree.

Then took she her sword and her target in hand,
And mounting the walls all undaunted did stand,
There daring their captains to match any three;
O, what a brave captain was Mary Ambree! 60

"Now say, English captain, what wouldest thou give
To ransom thyself, which else must not live?
Come yield thyself quickly or slain thou must be."
Then smilèd sweetly brave Mary Ambree.

"Ye captains courageous, of valour so bold,
Whom think you before you now you do behold?
No knight, sirs, of England, nor captain you see,
But a poor simple lass, called Mary Ambree."

"But art thou a woman as thou dost declare,
Whose valour hath proved so undaunted in war? 70
If England doth yield such brave lasses as thee,
Full well may they conquer, fair Mary Ambree!"

Then to her own country she back did return,
Still holding the foes of fair England in scorn;
Therefore English captains of every degree
Sing forth the brave valours of Mary Ambree.

Traditional Ballad.

BRAVE LORD WILLOUGHBY.

(158–)

The fifteenth day of July,
  With glistering spear and shield,
A famous fight in Flanders
  Was foughten in the field;
The most courageous officers
  Were English captains three,
But the bravest man in battle
  Was brave Lord Willoughby.

The next was Captain Norris,
  A valiant man was he; 10
The other, Captain Turner,
  From field would never flee.
With fifteen hundred fighting men—
  Alas, there were no more,—
They fought with fourteen thousand men
  Upon the bloody shore.

"Stand to it, noble pikemen,
  And look you round about!
And shoot you right, you bowmen,
  And we will keep them out! 20
You musquet and caliver men,
  Do you prove true to me;
I'll be the foremost man in fight!"
  Says brave Lord Willoughby.

And then the bloody enemy
  They fiercely did assail;
And fought it out most furiously,
  Not doubting to prevail.
The wounded men on both sides fell,
  Most piteous for to see, 30
Yet nothing could the courage quell
  Of brave Lord Willoughby.

For seven hours, to all men's view,
  The fight endurèd sore,
Until our men so feeble grew
  That they could fight no more.
And then upon dead horses
  Full savourly they ate,
And drank the puddle-water—
  They could no better get. 40

When they had fed so freely,
  They kneelèd on the ground,
And praisèd God devoutly
  For the favour they had found;
And beating up their colours,
  The fight they did renew,
And turning tow'rds the Spaniard,
  A thousand more they slew.

The sharp steel-pointed arrows
  And bullets thick did fly; 50
Then did our valiant soldiers
  Charge on most furiously;
Which made the Spaniards waver,
  They thought it best to flee;
They feared the stout behaviour
  Of brave Lord Willoughby.

And then the fearful enemy
  Was quickly put to flight;
Our men pursued courageously
  And caught their forces quite. 60
But at last they gave a shout
  Which echoed through the sky;
"God and Saint George for England!"
  The conquerors did cry.

This news was brought to England,
  With all the speed might be,
And soon our gracious Queen was told
  Of this same victory.
"O this is brave Lord Willoughby,
  My love that ever won; 70
Of all the Lords of honour
  'Tis he great deeds hath done."

To the soldiers that were maimèd
  And wounded in the fray,
The Queen allowed a pension
  Of fifteenpence a day:
And from all costs and charges
  She quit and set them free;
And this she did all for the sake
  Of brave Lord Willoughby. 80

Then, courage! noble Englishmen,
  And never be dismayed:
If that we be but one to ten
  We will not be afraid
To fight with foreign enemies,
  And set our nation free;
And thus I end the bloody bout
  Of brave Lord Willoughby.

Anon.

THE ARMADA.

(1588)

Attend, all ye who list to hear our noble England's praise;
I tell of the thrice famous deeds she wrought in ancient days,
When that great fleet invincible against her bore in vain
The richest spoils of Mexico, the stoutest hearts of Spain.

It was about the lovely close of a warm summer day,
There came a gallant merchant-ship full sail to Plymouth Bay;
Her crew hath seen Castile's black fleet, beyond Aurigny's isle,
At earliest twilight, on the waves lie heaving many a mile.
At sunrise she escaped their van, by God's especial grace;
And the tall Pinta, till the noon, had held her close in chase. 10
Forthwith a guard at every gun was placed along the wall;
The beacon blazed upon the roof of Edgecumbe's lofty hall;
Many a light fishing-bark put out to pry along the coast,
And with loose rein and bloody spur rode inland many a post.

With his white hair unbonneted, the stout old sheriff comes;
Behind him march the halberdiers; before him sound the drums;
His yeomen round the market cross make clear an ample space;
For there behoves him to set up the standard of Her Grace.
And haughtily the trumpets peal, and gaily dance the bells,
As slow upon the labouring wind the royal blazon swells. 20
Look how the Lion of the sea lifts up his ancient crown,
And underneath his deadly paw treads the gay lilies down!
So stalked he when he turned to flight on that famed Picard field
Bohemia's plume, and Genoa's bow, and Caesar's eagle shield.
So glared he when at Agincourt in wrath he turned to bay,
And crushed and torn beneath his claws the princely hunters lay.
Ho! strike the flagstaff deep, Sir Knight: ho! scatter flowers, fair maids:
Ho! gunners, fire a loud salute: ho! gallants, draw your blades:
Thou sun, shine on her joyously: ye breezes, waft her wide;
Our glorious SEMPER EADEM, the banner of our pride. 30

The freshening breeze of eve unfurled that banner's massy fold;
The parting gleam of sunshine kissed that haughty scroll of gold;
Night sank upon the dusky beach and on the purple sea,
Such night in England ne'er had been, nor e'er again shall be.
From Eddystone to Berwick bounds, from Lynn to Milford Bay,
That time of slumber was as bright and busy as the day;
For swift to east and swift to west the ghastly war-flame spread,
High on Saint Michael's Mount it shone: it shone on Beachy Head.
Far on the deep the Spaniard saw, along each southern shire,
Cape beyond cape, in endless range, those twinkling points of fire. 40
The fisher left his skiff to rock on Tamar's glittering waves:
The rugged miners poured to war from Mendip's sunless caves!
O'er Longleat's towers, o'er Cranbourne's oaks, the fiery herald flew:
He roused the shepherds of Stonehenge, the rangers of Beaulieu.
Right sharp and quick the bells all night rang out from Bristol town,
And ere the day three hundred horse had met on Clifton down;

The sentinel on Whitehall gate looked forth into the night,
And saw o'erhanging Richmond Hill the streak of blood-red light:
Then bugle's note and cannon's roar the death-like silence broke,
And with one start, and with one cry, the royal city woke. 50
At once on all her stately gates arose the answering fires;
At once the wild alarum clashed from all her reeling spires;
From all the batteries of the Tower pealed loud the voice of fear;
And all the thousand masts of Thames sent back a louder cheer;
And from the furthest wards was heard the rush of hurrying feet,
And the broad streams of pikes and flags rushed down each roaring street;
And broader still became the blaze, and louder still the din,
As fast from every village round the horse came spurring in.
And eastward straight from wild Blackheath the warlike errand went,
And roused in many an ancient hall the gallant squires of Kent. 60
Southward from Surrey's pleasant hills flew those bright couriers forth;
High on bleak Hampstead's swarthy moor they started for the north;

And on, and on, without a pause, untired they bounded still:
All night from tower to tower they sprang; they sprang from hill to hill:
Till the proud Peak unfurled the flag o'er Darwin's rocky dales,
Till like volcanoes flared to heaven the stormy hills of Wales,
Till twelve fair counties saw the blaze on Malvern's lonely height,
Till streamed in crimson on the wind the Wrekin's crest of light,
Till broad and fierce the star came forth on Ely's stately fane,
And tower and hamlet rose in arms o'er all the boundless plain; 70
Till Belvoir's lordly terraces the sign to Lincoln sent,
And Lincoln sped the message on o'er the wide vale of Trent;
Till Skiddaw saw the fire that burned on Gaunt's embattled pile,
And the red glare on Skiddaw roused the burghers of Carlisle.

LORD MACAULAY.

THE DEFEAT OF THE SPANISH ARMADA.

(1588)

Some years of late, in eighty-eight,
  As I do well remember,
It was, some say, the nineteenth of May,
  And some say in September,
  And some say in September.

The Spanish train launch'd forth amain,
  With many a fine bravado,
Their (as they thought, but it proved not)
  Invincible Armado,
  Invincible Armado. 10

There was a little man, that dwelt in Spain,
  Who shot well in a gun-a,
Don Pedro hight, as black a wight
  As the Knight of the Sun-a,
  As the Knight of the Sun-a.

King Philip made him admiral,
  And bid him not to stay-a,
But to destroy both man and boy,
  And so to come away-a,
  And so to come away-a. 20

Their navy was well victualled,
  With biscuit, pease and bacon;
They brought two ships, well fraught with whips,
  But I think they were mistaken,
  But I think they were mistaken.

Their men were young, munition strong,
  And, to do us more harm-a,
They thought it meet to join the fleet,
  All with the Prince of Parma,
  All with the Prince of Parma. 30

They coasted round about our land,
  And so came in by Dover;
But we had men set on 'um, then,
  And threw the rascals over,
  And threw the rascals over.

The Queen was then at Tilbury;
  What could we more desire-a?
And Sir Francis Drake, for her sweet sake,
  Did set them all on fire-a,
  Did set them all on fire-a. 40

Then straight they fled, by sea and land,
  That one man kill'd three score-a;
And had not they all ran away,
  In truth, he had kill'd more-a,
  In truth, he had kill'd more-a.

Then let them neither brag nor boast,
  But, if they come agen-a,
Let them take heed, they do not speed
  As they did, you know when-a,
  As they did, you know when-a. 50

Anon.

THE FAME OF SIR FRANCIS DRAKE.

(Drake d. 1595)

Sir Drake, whom well the world's end knew,
  Which thou did compass round,
And whom both poles of heaven once saw,
  Which north and south do bound;

The stars above would make thee known,
  If men here silent were;
The sun himself cannot forget
  His fellow-traveller.

Anon.

CAPTAIN WARD AND THE *RAINBOW*.

(c. 1605)

Strike up, you lusty gallants,
  With music and sound of drum,
For we have descried a rover,
  Upon the sea is come;
His name is Captain Ward,
  Right well it doth appear,
There has not been such a rover
  Found out this thousand year.

For he hath sent unto our king,
  The sixth of January, 10
Desiring that he might come in,
  With all his company;

"And if your king will let me come
  Till I my tale have told,
I will bestow for my ransom
  Full thirty ton of gold."

"O nay, O nay," then said our king,
  "O nay, this may not be,
To yield to such a rover,
  Myself will not agree; 20
He hath deceived the Frenchman,
  Likewise the King of Spain,
And how can he be true to me
  That hath been false to twain?"

With that our king provided
  A ship of worthy fame,
Rainbow she is called,
  If you would know her name;
Now the gallant Rainbow
  She rows upon the sea, 30
Five hundred gallant seamen
  To bear her company.

The Dutchman and the Spaniard
  She made them for to flee,
Also the bonny Frenchman,
  As she met him on the sea.
Whereas this gallant Rainbow
  Did come where Ward did lie,
"Where is the captain of this ship?"
  This gallant Rainbow did cry. 40

"O that am I," says Captain Ward,
  "There's no man bids me lie,
And if thou art the king's fair ship,
  Thou art welcome unto me."
"I'll tell thee what," says Rainbow,
  "Our king is in great grief
That thou shouldst lie upon the sea
  And play the arrant thief;

"And will not let our merchants' ships
  Pass as they did before; 50
Such tidings to our king is come,
  Which grieves his heart full sore."
With that this gallant Rainbow,
  She shot, out of her pride,
Full fifty gallant brass pieces,
  Chargèd on every side.

And yet these gallant shooters
  Prevailèd not a pin;
Though they were brass on the outside,
  Brave Ward was steel within; 60
"Shoot on, shoot on," says Captain Ward,
  "Your sport well pleaseth me,
And he that first gives over
  Shall yield unto the sea.

"I never wronged an English ship,
  But Turk and King of Spain,
For and the jovial Dutchman
  As I met on the main.

If I had known your king
  But one-two years before, 70
I would have saved brave Essex' life,
  Whose death did grieve me sore.

"Go tell the King of England,
  Go tell him thus from me,
If he reign king of all the land,
  I will reign king at sea."
With that the gallant Rainbow shot,
  And shot, and shot in vain,
And left the rover's company,
  And returned home again. 80

"Our royal King of England,
  Your ship's returned again,
For Ward's ship is so strong
  It never will be ta'en."
"O everlasting!" says our king,
  "I have lost jewels three,
Which would have gone unto the seas
  And brought proud Ward to me.

"The first was Lord Clifford,
  Earl of Cumberland; 90
The second was the Lord Mountjoy,
  As you shall understand;
The third was brave Essex,
  From field would never flee;
Which would 'a' gone unto the seas,
  And brought proud Ward to me."

Traditional Ballad.

WHEN THE KING ENJOYS HIS OWN AGAIN.

(1643)

What Booker can prognosticate,
Concerning kings or kingdom's fate?
I think myself to be as wise
As he that gazeth on the skies:
My skill goes beyond
The depths of a Pond
Or Rivers in the greatest rain;
Whereby I can tell,
All things will be well,
When the King enjoys his own again. 10

There's neither Swallow, Dove, nor Dade
Can soar more high, nor deeper wade;
Nor show a reason from the stars,
What causeth peace or civil wars;
The man in the moon
May wear out his shoon,
By running after Charles his wain;
But all's to no end,
For the times will not mend
Till the King enjoys his own again. 20

Though for a time we see Whitehall
With cobwebs hanging on the wall,
Instead of silk and silver wave,
Which formerly it used to have;
With rich perfume
In every room,

Delightful to that princely train,
Which again you shall see,
When the time it shall be
That the King enjoys his own again. 30

Full forty years the royal crown
Hath been his father's and his own;
And is there anyone but he,
That in the same should sharer be?
For who better may
The sceptre sway,
Than he that hath such right to reign?
Then let's hope for a peace,
For the wars will not cease,
Till the King enjoys his own again. 40

Till then upon Ararat's hill
My Hope shall cast her anchor still,
Until I see some peaceful dove
Bring home the branch I dearly love:
Then will I wait
Till the waters abate,
Which now disturb my troubled brain,
Else never rejoice
Till I hear the voice,
That the King enjoys his own again. 50

MARTIN PARKER.

SIR NICHOLAS AT MARSTON MOOR.

(1644)

To horse! to horse, Sir Nicholas, the clarion's note is
high!
To horse! to horse, Sir Nicholas, the big drum makes
reply!
Ere this hath Lucas marched, with his gallant
cavaliers,
And the bray of Rupert's trumpets grows fainter on
our ears.
To horse! to horse! Sir Nicholas! White Guy is at the
door,
And the vulture whets his beak o'er the field of
Marston Moor.

Up rose the Lady Alice from her brief and broken
prayer,
And she brought a silken standard down the narrow
turret-stair;
Oh! many were the tears that those radiant eyes had
shed,
As she worked the bright word "Glory" in the gay
and glancing thread; 10
And mournful was the smile which o'er those beau-
teous features ran,
As she said: "It is your lady's gift; unfurl it in the
van!"

"It shall flutter, noble wench, where the best and boldest ride,
Thro' the steel-clad files of Skippon, the black dragoons of Pride;
The recreant soul of Fairfax will feel a sicklier qualm,
And the rebel lips of Oliver give out a louder psalm,
When they see my lady's gewgaw flaunt bravely on their wing,
And hear her loyal soldiers' shout, For God and for the King!"

'Tis noon. The ranks are broken, along the royal line
They fly, the braggarts of the court! the bullies of the Rhine! 20
Stout Langley's cheer is heard no more, and Astley's helm is down,
And Rupert sheathes his rapier with a curse and with a frown,
And cold Newcastle mutters, as he follows in the flight,
"The German boar had better far have supped in York to-night."

The knight is all alone, his steel cap cleft in twain,
His good buff jerkin crimsoned o'er with many a gory stain;
Yet still he waves the standard, and cries amid the rout,
"For Church and King, fair gentlemen! spur on, and fight it out!"
And now he wards a Roundhead's pike, and now he hums a stave,
And here he quotes a stage-play, and there he fells a knave. 30

God speed to thee, Sir Nicholas! thou hast no thought of fear;
God speed to thee, Sir Nicholas! but fearful odds are here!
The traitors ring thee round, and with every blow and thrust,
"Down, down," they cry, "with Belial! down with him to the dust!"
"I would," quoth grim old Oliver, "that Belial's trusty sword
This day were doing battle for the Saints and for the Lord!"

The Lady Alice sits with her maidens in her bower,
The grey-haired warden watches from the castle's highest tower;
"What news? what news, old Anthony?"—"The field is lost and won:
The ranks of war are melting as the mists beneath the sun! 40
And a wounded man speeds hither—I'm old and cannot see,
Or sure I am that sturdy step my master's step should be!"

"I bring thee back the standard from as rude and rough a fray
As e'er was proof of soldier's thews, or theme for minstrel's lay!
Bid Hubert fetch the silver bowl, and liquor *quantum suff.*;
I'll make a shift to drain it, ere I part with boot and buff—

Though Guy through many a gaping wound is
breathing out his life,
And I come to thee a landless man, my fond and
faithful wife.

"Sweet! we will fill our money-bags, and freight a
ship for France,
And mourn in merry Paris for this poor realm's
mischance: 50
Or if the worst betide me, why better axe or rope,
Than life with Lenthall for a king, and Peters for a
pope!
Alas! alas! my gallant Guy!—out on the crop-eared
boor
That sent me, with my standard, on foot from Marston
Moor!"

W. M. Praed.

THE BATTLE OF NASEBY.

(1645)

Oh, wherefore come ye forth in triumph from the
north,
With your hands, and your feet, and your raiment
all red?
And wherefore doth your rout send forth a joyous
shout?
And whence be the grapes of the wine-press which
ye tread?

Oh, evil was the root, and bitter was the fruit,
And crimson was the juice of the vintage that we trod;
For we trampled on the throng of the haughty and the strong,
Who sate in the high places, and slew the saints of God.

It was about the noon of a glorious day of June,
That we saw their banners dance, and their cuirasses shine, 10
And the Man of Blood was there, with his long essenced hair,
And Astley, and Sir Marmaduke, and Rupert of the Rhine.

Like a servant of the Lord, with his Bible and his sword,
The general rode along us to form us to the fight,
When a murmuring sound broke out, and swelled into a shout,
Among the godless horsemen upon the tyrant's right.

And hark! like the roar of the billows on the shore,
The cry of battle rises along their charging line!
For God! for the Cause! for the Church! for the Laws!
For Charles King of England, and Rupert of the Rhine! 20

The furious German comes, with his clarions and his drums,
His bravoes of Alsatia and pages of Whitehall;
They are bursting on our flanks. Grasp your pikes, close your ranks;
For Rupert never comes but to conquer or to fall.

They are here! They rush on! We are broken! We are gone!
Our left is borne before them like stubble on the blast.
O Lord, put forth thy might! O Lord, defend the right!
Stand back to back, in God's name, and fight it to the last.

Stout Skippon hath a wound; the centre hath given ground.
Hark! hark! What means the trampling of horsemen on our rear? 30
Whose banner do I see, boys? 'Tis he, thank God, 'tis he, boys.
Bear up another minute: brave Oliver is here.

Their heads all stooping low, their points all in a row,
Like a whirlwind on the trees, like a deluge on the dykes,
Our cuirassiers have burst on the ranks of the Accurst,
And at a shock have scattered the forest of his pikes.

Fast, fast, the gallants ride, in some safe nook to hide
Their coward heads, predestined to rot on Temple Bar,
And he—he turns, he flies:—shame on those cruel eyes
That bore to look on torture, and dare not look on war! 40

Ho! comrades, scour the plain; and, ere ye strip the slain,
First give another stab to make your search secure;
Then shake from sleeves and pockets their broad-pieces and lockets,
The tokens of the wanton, the plunder of the poor.

Fools! your doublets shone with gold, and your hearts were gay and bold,
When you kissed your lily hands to your lemans to-day;
And to-morrow shall the fox, from her chambers in the rocks,
Lead forth her tawny cubs to howl above the prey.

Where be your tongues that late mocked at heaven and hell and fate,
And the fingers that once were so busy with your blades, 50
Your perfumed satin clothes, your catches and your oaths,
Your stage-plays and your sonnets, your diamonds and your spades?

Down, down, for ever down with the mitre and the crown,
With the Belial of the Court, and the Mammon of the Pope;
There is woe in Oxford halls; there is wail in Durham's stalls;
The Jesuit smites his bosom; the bishop rends his cope.

And she of the seven hills shall mourn her children's ills,
And tremble when she thinks on the edge of England's sword;
And the kings of earth in fear shall shudder when they hear
What the hand of God hath wrought for the Houses and the Word. 60

LORD MACAULAY.

ON THE LORD GENERAL FAIRFAX AT THE SIEGE OF COLCHESTER.

(1648)

Fairfax, whose name in arms through Europe rings,
Filling each mouth with envy or with praise,
And all her jealous monarchs with amaze,
And rumours loud that daunt remotest kings,
Thy firm unshaken virtue ever brings
Victory home, though new rebellions raise
Their Hydra heads, and the false North displays
Her broken league to imp their serpent wings.
O yet a nobler task awaits thy hand
(For what can war but endless war still breed?) 10
Till truth and right from violence be freed,
And public faith cleared from the shameful brand
Of public fraud. In vain doth Valour bleed,
While Avarice and Rapine share the land.

JOHN MILTON.

AN HORATIAN ODE UPON CROMWELL'S RETURN FROM IRELAND.

(1650)

The forward youth that would appear,
Must now forsake his Muses dear,
    Nor in the shadows sing
    His numbers languishing.

'Tis time to leave the books in dust,
And oil the unusèd armour's rust,
    Removing from the wall
    The corslet of the hall.

So restless Cromwell could not cease
In the inglorious arts of peace, 10
    But through adventurous war
    Urgèd his active star:

And like the three-fork'd lightning, first
Breaking the clouds where it was nurst,
    Did thorough his own Side
    His fiery way divide:

For 'tis all one to courage high,
The emulous, or enemy;
    And with such, to enclose
    Is more than to oppose; 20

Then burning through the air he went
And palaces and temples rent;
    And Caesar's head at last
    Did through his laurels blast.

'Tis madness to resist or blame
The face of angry heaven's flame;
    And if we would speak true,
    Much to the Man is due

Who, from his private gardens, where
He lived reservèd and austere, 30
    (As if his highest plot
    To plant the bergamot,)

Could by industrious valour climb
To ruin the great work of time
    And cast the Kingdoms old
    Into another mould;

Though Justice against Fate complain,
And plead the ancient Rights in vain—
    But those do hold or break
    As men are strong or weak; 40

Nature, that hateth emptiness,
Allows of penetration less,
    And therefore must make room
    Where greater spirits come.

What field of all the civil war
Where his were not the deepest scar?
    And Hampton shows what part
    He had of wiser art,

Where, twining subtle fears with hope,
He wove a net of such a scope 50
    That Charles himself might chase
    To Carisbrook's narrow case,

That thence the Royal actor borne
The tragic scaffold might adorn:
While round the armèd bands
Did clap their bloody hands.

He nothing common did or mean
Upon that memorable scene,
But with his keener eye
The axe's edge did try; 60

Nor call'd the Gods, with vulgar spite,
To vindicate his helpless right;
But bow'd his comely head
Down, as upon a bed.

—This was that memorable hour
Which first assured the forcèd power:
So when they did design
The Capitol's first line,

A Bleeding Head, where they begun,
Did fright the architects to run; 70
And yet in that the State
Foresaw its happy fate!

And now the Irish are ashamed
To see themselves in one year tamed:
So much one man can do
That does both act and know.

They can affirm his praises best,
And have, though overcome, confest
How good he is, how just
And fit for highest trust. 80

Nor yet grown stiffer with command,
But still in the Republic's hand—
How fit he is to sway
That can so well obey!

He to the Common's feet presents
A Kingdom for his first year's rents,
And (what he may) forbears
His fame, to make it theirs:

And has his sword and spoils ungirt
To lay them at the Public's skirt. 90
So when the falcon high
Falls heavy from the sky,

She, having kill'd, no more doth search
But on the next green bough to perch,
Where, when he first does lure,
The falconer has her sure.

—What may not then our Isle presume
While Victory his crest does plume?
What may not others fear
If thus he crowns each year? 100

As Caesar he, ere long, to Gaul,
To Italy an Hannibal,
And to all States not free
Shall climacteric be.

The Pict no shelter now shall find
Within his parti-colour'd mind,
But from this valour sad
Shrink underneath the plaid—

Happy, if in the tufted brake
The English hunter him mistake 110
Nor lay his hounds in near
The Caledonian deer.

But thou, the War's and Fortune's son,
March indefatigably on;
And for the last effect
Still keep the sword erect:

Besides the force it has to fright
The spirits of the shady night,
The same arts that did gain
A power, must it maintain. 120

ANDREW MARVELL.

TO CROMWELL.

(1652)

Cromwell, our chief of men, who through a cloud
Not of war only, but detractions rude,
Guided by faith and matchless fortitude,
To peace and truth thy glorious way hast ploughed,
And on the neck of crownèd Fortune proud
Hast reared God's trophies, and his work pursued;
While Darwen stream, with blood of Scots imbrued,
And Dunbar field, resounds thy praises loud,
And Worcester's laureate wreath: yet much remains
To conquer still; Peace hath her victories 10
No less renowned than War: new foes arise,
Threatening to bind our souls with secular chains.
Help us to save free conscience from the paw
Of hireling wolves, whose Gospel is their maw.

JOHN MILTON.

THE FIRE OF LONDON

(*selected from "Annus Mirabilis"*).

(1666)

Swell'd with our late successes on the foe,
  Which France and Holland wanted power to cross,
We urge an unseen fate to lay us low,
  And feed their envious eyes with English loss.

Each element His dread command obeys,
  Who makes or ruins with a smile or frown;
Who, as by one He did our nation raise,
  So now He with another pulls us down.

Yet, London! empress of the northern clime,
  By an high fate thou greatly didst expire; 10
Great as the world's, which, at the death of Time,
  Must fall, and rise a nobler frame by fire.

As when some dire usurper heaven provides,
  To scourge his country with a lawless sway;
His birth, perhaps, some petty village hides,
  And sets his cradle out of fortune's way:

Till fully ripe his swelling fate breaks out,
  And hurries him to mighty mischiefs on;
His prince, surprised at first, no ill could doubt,
  And wants the power to meet it when 'tis known: 20

Such was the rise of this prodigious Fire,
  Which in mean buildings first obscurely bred,
From thence did soon to open streets aspire,
  And straight to palaces and temples spread.

The diligence of trades and noiseful gain,
  And luxury, more late, asleep was laid;
All was the Night's, and in her silent reign
  No sound the rest of Nature did invade.

In this deep quiet, from what source unknown,
  Those seeds of fire their fatal birth disclose; 30
And first few scattering sparks about were blown
  Big with the flames that to our ruin rose.

Then in some close-pent room it crept along
  And, smouldering as it went, in silence fed;
Till the infant monster, with devouring strong,
  Walk'd boldly upright with exalted head.

Now like some rich and mighty murderer,
  Too great for prison, which he breaks with gold,
Who fresher for new mischiefs doth appear
  And dares the world to tax him with the old, 40

So scapes the insulting fire his narrow jail
  And makes small outlets into open air;
There the fierce winds his tender force assail
  And beat him downward to his first repair.

And now, no longer letted of his prey,
  He leaps up at it with enraged desire,
O'erlooks the neighbours with a wide survey,
  And nods at every house his threatening fire.

The ghosts of traitors from the Bridge descend,
  With bold fanatic spectres to rejoice; 50
About the fire into a dance they bend,
  And sing their Sabbath notes with feeble voice.

Our guardian angel saw them where they sate,
  Above the palace of our slumbering king;
He sigh'd, abandoning his charge to Fate,
  And drooping, oft looked back upon the wing.

At length the crackling noise and dreadful blaze
  Call'd up some waking lover to the sight;
And long it was ere he the rest could raise
  Whose heavy eyelids yet were full of night. 60

The next to danger, hot pursued by fate,
  Half-clothed, half-naked, hastily retire;
And frighted mothers strike their breasts too late,
  For helpless infants left amidst the fire.

Their cries soon waken all the dwellers near;
  Now murmuring noises rise in every street;
The more remote run stumbling with their fear,
  And in the dark men jostle as they meet.

Now streets grow throng'd, and busy as by day:
  Some run for buckets to the hallowed quire; 70
Some cut the pipes, and some the engines play,
  And some, more bold, mount ladders to the fire.

Old father Thames raised up his reverend head,
  But fear'd the fate of Simois would return;
Deep in his ooze he sought his sedgy bed,
  And shrunk his waters back into his urn.

The fire, meantime, walks in a broader gross;
  To either hand his wings he opens wide;
He wades the streets, and straight he reaches 'cross,
  And plays his longing flames on th' other side. 80

At first they warm, then scorch, and then they take;
  Now with long necks from side to side they feed;
At length, grown strong, their mother-fire forsake,
  And a new colony of flames succeed.

Now day appears, and with the day the king,
  Whose early care had robb'd him of his rest;
Far off the cracks of falling houses ring,
  And shrieks of subjects pierce his tender breast.

Himself directs what first is to be done,
  And orders all the succours which they bring; 90
The helpful and the good about him run,
  And form an army worthy such a king.

No help avails; for, Hydra-like, the Fire
  Lifts up his hundred heads to aim his way;
And scarce the wealthy can one half retire,
  Before he rushes in to share the prey.

At length the Almighty cast a pitying eye,
  And mercy softly touch'd his melting breast;
He saw the town's one half in rubbish lie,
  And eager flames drive on to storm the rest. 100

The vanquish'd fires withdraw from every place,
  Or, full with feeding, sink into a sleep:
Each household genius shows again his face,
  And from the hearths the little Lares creep.

Methinks already from this chemic flame,
  I see a city of more precious mould;
Rich as the town which gives the Indies name,
  With silver paved, and all divine with gold.

Already labouring with a mighty fate,
  She shakes the rubbish from her mountain brow, 110
And seems to have renew'd her charter's date,
  Which heaven will to the death of Time allow.

More great than human now, and more august,
  Now deified she from her fires does rise;
Her widening streets on new foundations trust,
  And opening into larger parts she flies.

Before, she like some shepherdess did show,
  Who sat to bathe her by a river's side;
Not answering to her fame, but rude and low,
  Nor taught the beauteous arts of modern pride. 120

Now, like a Maiden Queen, she will behold,
  From her high turrets, hourly suitors come;
The East with incense, and the West with gold,
  Will stand like suppliants to receive her doom.

The silver Thames, her own domestic flood,
  Shall bear her vessels like a sweeping train;
And often wind, as of his mistress proud,
  With longing eyes to meet her face again.

JOHN DRYDEN.

THE SONG OF THE WESTERN MEN.

(1688)

A good sword and a trusty hand,
  A merry heart and true!
King James's men shall understand
  What Cornishmen can do.

And have they fixed the where and when
  And shall Trelawney die?
Then twenty thousand Cornish men
  Will know the reason why!

Out spake the captain, brave and bold,—
  A merry wight was he; 10
Though London Tower were Michael's hold,
  We'll set Trelawney free.

We'll cross the Tamar, land to land,
  The Severn is no stay;
And side by side, and hand in hand,
  And who shall bid us nay?

And when we come to London wall,
  A pleasant sight to view;—
Come forth, come forth, ye cowards, all;
  Here are better men than you! 20

Trelawney he's in keep in hold,
  Trelawney he may die,
But twenty thousand Cornish bold
  Will know the reason why!

R. S. HAWKER.

THE BURIAL MARCH OF DUNDEE.

(Battle of Killiecrankie, 1689)

On the heights of Killiecrankie
  Yester-morn our army lay;
Slowly rose the mist in columns
  From the river's broken way;
Hoarsely roared the swollen torrent,
  And the Pass was wrapped in gloom,
When the clansmen rose together
  From their lair amidst the broom.
Then we belted on our tartans,
  And our bonnets down we drew, 10
And we felt our broadswords' edges,
  And we proved them to be true;
And we prayed the prayer of soldiers,
  And we cried the gathering-cry,
And we clasped the hands of kinsmen
  And we swore to do or die!
Then our leader rode before us
  On his war-horse black as night—
Well the Cameronian rebels
  Knew that charger in the fight! 20
And a cry of exultation
  From the bearded warriors rose;
For we loved the house of Claver'se,
  And we thought of good Montrose.
But he raised his hand for silence—
  "Soldiers! I have sworn a vow;
Ere the evening-star shall glisten
  On Schehallion's lofty brow,

Either we shall rest in triumph,
  Or another of the Græmes 30
Shall have died in battle-harness
  For his country and King James!
Think upon the Royal Martyr—
  Think of what his race endure—
Think on him whom butchers murder'd
  On the field of Magus Muir:—
By his sacred blood I charge ye—
  By the ruin'd hearth and shrine—
By the blighted hopes of Scotland—
  By your injuries and mine— 40
Strike this day as if the anvil
  Lay beneath your blows the while,
Be they Covenanting traitors,
  Or the brood of false Argyle!
Strike! and drive the trembling rebels
  Backwards o'er the stormy Forth;
Let them tell their pale Convention
  How they fared within the North.
Let them tell that Highland honour
  Is not to be bought nor sold— 50
That we scorn their Prince's anger,
  As we loathe his foreign gold.
Strike! and when the fight is over,
  If ye look in vain for me,
Where the dead are lying thickest,
  Search for him that was Dundee!"

Loudly then the hills re-echoed
  With our answer to his call,
But a deeper echo sounded
  In the bosoms of us all. 60

For the lands of wide Breadalbane
  Not a man who heard him speak
Would that day have left the battle.
  Burning eye and flushing cheek
Told the clansmen's fierce emotion,
  And they harder drew their breath;
For their souls were strong within them,
  Stronger than the grasp of death.
Soon we heard a challenge-trumpet
  Sounding in the Pass below, 70
And the distant tramp of horses,
  And the voices of the foe:
Down we crouched amid the bracken,
  Till the Lowland ranks drew near,
Panting like the hounds in summer
  When they scent the stately deer.
From the dark defile emerging,
  Next we saw the squadrons come,
Leslie's foot and Leven's troopers
  Marching to the tuck of drum; 80
Through the scattered wood of birches,
  O'er the broken ground and heath,
Wound the long battalion slowly,
  Till they gained the field beneath;
Then we bounded from our covert!
  Judge how looked the Saxons then,
When they saw the rugged mountain
  Start to life with armèd men!
Like a tempest down the ridges
  Swept the hurricane of steel— 90
Rose the slogan of Macdonald,
  Flashed the broadsword of Locheill!
Vainly sped the withering volley
  'Mongst the foremost of our band;

On we poured, until we met them—
  Foot to foot, and hand to hand!
Horse and man went down like driftwood
  When the floods are black at Yule,
And their carcasses are whirling
  In the Garry's deepest pool. 100
Horse and man went down before us;
  Living foe there tarried none
On the field of Killiecrankie,
  When that stubborn fight was done!

And the evening-star was shining
  On Schehallion's distant head,
When we wiped our bloody broadswords,
  And returned to count the dead.
There we found him, gashed and gory
  Stretch'd upon the cumbered plain, 110
As he told us where to seek him—
  In the thickest of the slain.
And a smile was on his visage,
  For within his dying ear
Pealed the joyful note of triumph,
  And the clansmen's clamorous cheer:
So, amidst the battle's thunder,
  Shot, and steel, and scorching flame,
In the glory of his manhood
  Passed the spirit of the Græme! 120

Open wide the vaults of Athol,
  Where the bones of heroes rest—
Open wide the hallowed portals
  To receive another guest!

Last of Scots and last of freemen—
  Last of all that dauntless race
Who would rather die unsullied
  Than outlive the land's disgrace!
Oh, thou lion-hearted warrior!
  Reck not of the after-time: 130
Honour may be deemed dishonour,
  Loyalty be called a crime.
Sleep in peace with kindred ashes
  Of the noble and the true,
Hands that never failed their country,
  Hearts that never baseness knew.
Sleep!—and till the latest trumpet
  Wakes the dead from earth and sea,
Scotland shall not boast a braver
  Chieftain than our own Dundee! 140

W. E. AYTOUN.

ADMIRAL BENBOW.

(1702)

O, we sail'd to Virginia, and thence to Fayal,
Where we water'd our shipping, and then we weigh'd
  all;
Full in view on the seas, boys, seven sails we did
  espy;
O, we mannèd our capstan, and weigh'd speedily.

The first we came up with was a brigantine sloop,
And we ask'd if the others were as big as they
  look'd;
But turning to windward as near as we could lie,
We found there were ten men-of-war cruising by.

O, we drew up our squadron in very nice line,
And boldly we fought them for full four hours'
time; 10
But the day being spent, boys, and night coming on,
We let them alone till the very next morn.

The very next morning the engagement proved hot,
And brave Admiral Benbow received a chain-shot;
And when he was wounded, to his men he did say,
"Take me up in your arms, boys, and carry me away."

O, the guns they did rattle, and the bullets did fly,
But Admiral Benbow for help would not cry;
"Take me down to the cock-pit, there is ease for my
smarts,
If my merry men see me, it will sure break their
hearts." 20

The very next morning, by break of the day,
They hoisted their topsails, and so bore away;
We bore to Port Royal, where the people flocked
much
To see Admiral Benbow carried to Kingston Church.

Come, all you brave fellows, wherever you've been,
Let us drink to the health of our king and our queen,
And another good health to the girls that we know,
And a third in remembrance of brave Admiral
Benbow.

Anon.

AFTER BLENHEIM.

(1704)

It was a summer evening,
  Old Kaspar's work was done,
And he before his cottage door
  Was sitting in the sun,
And by him sported on the green
His little grandchild Wilhelmine.

She saw her brother Peterkin
  Roll something large and round,
Which he beside the rivulet
  In playing there had found; 10
He came to ask what he had found
That was so large and smooth and round.

Old Kaspar took it from the boy
  Who stood expectant by;
And then the old man shook his head,
  And with a natural sigh—
"'Tis some poor fellow's skull," said he,
"Who fell in the great victory."

"I find them in the garden,
  For there's many here about; 20
And often when I go to plough
  The ploughshare turns them out.
For many a thousand men," said he,
"Were slain in that great victory."

"Now tell us what 'twas all about,"
  Young Peterkin he cries:
And little Wilhelmine looks up
  With wonder-waiting eyes;
"Now tell us all about the war,
And what they fought each other for." 30

"It was the English," Kaspar cried,
  "Who put the French to rout;
But what they fought each other for
  I could not well make out.
But every body said," quoth he,
"That 'twas a famous victory.

"My father lived at Blenheim then,
  Yon little stream hard by;
They burnt his dwelling to the ground,
  And he was forced to fly: 40
So with his wife and child he fled,
Nor had he where to rest his head.

"With fire and sword the country round
  Was wasted far and wide,
And many a childing mother then
  And new-born baby died:
But things like that, you know, must be
At every famous victory.

"They say it was a shocking sight
  After the field was won; 50
For many thousand bodies here
  Lay rotting in the sun;
But things like that, you know, must be
After a famous victory.

"Great praise the Duke of Marlbro' won,
And our good Prince Eugene."
"Why, 'twas a very wicked thing!"
Said little Wilhelmine.
"Nay, nay, my little girl," quoth he,
"It was a famous victory. 60

"And every body praised the Duke
Who this great fight did win."
"But what good came of it at last?"
Quoth little Peterkin.
"Why that I cannot tell," said he,
"But 'twas a famous victory."

ROBERT SOUTHEY.

THE VICAR OF BRAY.

(c. 1720)

In good King Charles's golden days,
When loyalty no harm meant,
A zealous High-Churchman was I,
And so I got preferment.
To teach my flock I never miss'd
Kings were by God appointed;
And lost are those that dare resist
Or touch the Lord's anointed.

And this is law that I'll maintain
Until my dying day, sir: 10
That whatsoever king shall reign,
I'll be the Vicar of Bray, sir.

When royal James possess'd the crown,
  And Popery grew in fashion,
The penal laws I hooted down,
  And read the Declaration.
The Church of Rome I found would fit
  Full well my constitution;
And I had been a Jesuit,
  But for the Revolution. 20

   And this is law, etc.

When William was our King declared
  To ease the nation's grievance,
With this new wind about I steer'd
  And swore to him allegiance.
Old principles I did revoke,
  Set conscience at a distance;
Passive obedience was a joke,
  A jest was non-resistance.

   And this is law, etc.

When royal Anne became our Queen,
  The Church of England's glory, 30
Another face of things was seen,
  And I became a Tory,
Occasional conformists base,
  I blamed their moderation;
And thought the Church in danger was
  By such prevarication.

   And this is law, etc.

When George in pudding-time came o'er,
  And moderate men look'd big, sir,
My principles I changed once more,
  And so became a Whig, sir. 40
And thus preferment I procured
  From our new faith's defender;
And almost every day abjured
  The Pope and the Pretender.

    And this is law, etc.

Th' illustrious house of Hanover
  And Protestant succession,
To them I do allegiance swear—
  While they can keep possession;
For in my faith and loyalty
  I never more will falter, 50
And George my lawful king shall be—
  Until the times do alter.

    And this is law, etc.

Anon.

A BALLAD OF THE BOSTON TEA-PARTY.

(1773)

No! never such a draught was poured
  Since Hebe served with nectar
The bright Olympians and their Lord,
  Her over-kind protector,—
Since Father Noah squeezed the grape,
  And took to such behaving
As would have shamed our grandsire ape
  Before the days of shaving;
No! ne'er was mingled such a draught
  In palace, hall, or arbour, 10
As freemen brewed and tyrants quaffed
  That night in Boston Harbour!

It kept King George so long awake
  His brain at last got addled,
It made the nerves of Britain shake,
  With sevenscore millions saddled:
Before that bitter cup was drained,
  Amid the roar of cannon,
The Western war-cloud's crimson stained
  The Thames, the Clyde, the Shannon; 20
Full many a six-foot grenadier
  The flattened grass had measured,
And many a mother many a year
  Her tearful memories treasured;
Fast spread the tempest's darkening pall,
  The mighty realms were troubled,
The storm broke loose—but first of all
  The Boston tea-pot bubbled!

An evening party,—only that,
No formal invitation, 30
No gold-laced coat, no stiff cravat,
No feast in contemplation,
No silk-robed dames, no fiddling band,
No flowers, no songs, no dancing—
A tribe of Red men, axe in hand,
Behold the guests advancing!

How fast the stragglers join the throng,
From stall and workshop gathered!
The lively barber skips along
And leaves a chin half-lathered; 40
The smith has flung his hammer down,
The horse-shoe still is glowing;
The truant tapster at the Crown
Has left a beer-cask flowing;
The cooper's boys have dropped the adze,
And trot behind their master;
Up run the tarry ship-yard lads,
The crowd is hurrying faster.—
Out from the mill-pond's purlieus gush
The streams of white-faced millers, 50
And down their slippery alleys rush
The lusty young Fort-Hillers;
The rope-walk lends its prentice crew,—
The tories seize the omen;
"Ay, boys, you'll soon have work to do,
For England's rebel foemen,
King Hancock, Adams, and their gang,
That fire the mob with treason,—
When these we shoot and those we hang,
The town will come to reason." 60

On, on to where the tea-ships ride!
  And now their ranks are forming,—
A rush, and up the Dartmouth's side
  The Mohawk band is swarming!
See the fierce natives! What a glimpse
  Of paint, and fur, and feather,
As all at once the full-grown imps
  Light on the deck together!
A scarf the pig-tail's secret keeps,
  A blanket hides the breeches, 70
And out the cursed cargo leaps
  And overboard it pitches!

A woman, at the evening board
  So gracious, sweet, and purring,
So happy while the tea is poured,
  So blest while spoons are stirring,—
What martyr can compare with thee,
  The mother, wife, or daughter,
That night, instead of best Bohea,
  Condemned to milk and water! 80
Ah, little dreams the quiet dame
  Who plies with rock and spindle
The patient flax, how great a flame
  Yon little spark shall kindle!
The lurid morning shall reveal
  A fire no king can smother,
Where British flint and Boston steel
  Have dashed against each other!
Old charters shrivel in its track,
  His worship's bench has crumbled, 90
It climbs and clasps the union-jack,
  Its blazoned pomp is humbled;

The flags go down on land and sea,
  Like corn before the reapers;
So burned the fire that brewed the tea,
  That Boston served her keepers!

The waves that wrought a century's wreck
  Have rolled o'er Whig and Tory;
The Mohawks on the Dartmouth's deck
  Still live in song and story; 100
The waters in the rebel bay
  Have kept their tea-leaf savour;
Our old North-enders in their spray
  Still taste a Hyson flavour;
And freedom's tea-cup still o'erflows
  With ever-fresh libations,
To cheat of slumber all her foes
  And cheer the wakening nations!

O. W. HOLMES.

THE LOSS OF THE *ROYAL GEORGE*.

(1782)

Toll for the brave,
  The brave that are no more!
All sunk beneath the wave
  Fast by their native shore!

Eight hundred of the brave,
  Whose courage well was tried,
Had made the vessel heel,
  And laid her on her side.

A land breeze shook the shrouds,
  And she was overset; 10
Down went the *Royal George*,
  With all her crew complete!

Toll for the brave!
  Brave Kempenfelt is gone,
His last sea-fight is fought,
  His work of glory done.

It was not in the battle;
  No tempest gave the shock;
She sprang no fatal leak;
  She ran upon no rock. 20

His sword was in its sheath,
  His fingers held the pen,
When Kempenfelt went down
  With twice four hundred men.

Weigh the vessel up,
  Once dreaded by our foes!
And mingle with our cup
  The tears that England owes.

Her timbers yet are sound,
  And she may float again, 30
Full charged with England's thunder,
  And plough the distant main.

But Kempenfelt is gone,
  His victories are o'er;
And he and his eight hundred
  Shall plough the wave no more.

WILLIAM COWPER.

THE BATTLE OF THE BALTIC.

(1801)

Of Nelson and the North
Sing the glorious day's renown,
When to battle fierce came forth
All the might of Denmark's crown,
And her arms along the deep proudly shone,
By each gun the lighted brand,
In a bold determined hand,
And the Prince of all the land
Led them on.

Like leviathans afloat 10
Lay their bulwarks on the brine;
While the sign of battle flew
On the lofty British line:
It was ten of April morn by the chime:
As they drifted on their path
There was silence deep as death;
And the boldest held his breath
For a time.

But the might of England flushed
To anticipate the scene; 20
And her van the fleeter rushed
O'er the deadly space between.
"Hearts of oak!" our captains cried, when each gun
From its adamantine lips
Spread a death-shade round the ships,
Like the hurricane eclipse
Of the sun.

Again! again! again!
And the havoc did not slack,
Till a feeble cheer the Dane 30
To our cheering sent us back;—
Their shots along the deep slowly boom:—
Then ceased—and all is wail,
As they strike the shattered sail;
Or in conflagration pale
Light the gloom.

Out spoke the victor then
As he hailed them o'er the wave,
"Ye are brothers! ye are men!
And we conquer but to save: 40
So peace instead of death let us bring;
But yield, proud foe, thy fleet
With the crews, at England's feet,
And make submission meet
To our King."

Then Denmark blessed our chief
That he gave her wounds repose;
And the sounds of joy and grief
From her people wildly rose,
As death withdrew his shades from the day: 50
While the sun looked smiling bright
O'er a wide and woeful sight,
Where the fires of funeral light
Died away.

Now joy, Old England, raise
For the tidings of thy might,
By the festal cities' blaze,
Whilst the wine-cup shines in light;

And yet amidst that joy and uproar,
Let us think of them that sleep 60
Full many a fathom deep
By thy wild and stormy steep,
Elsinore!

Brave hearts! to Britain's pride
Once so faithful and so true,
On the deck of fame that died
With the gallant good Riou;
Soft sigh the winds of Heaven o'er their grave!
While the billow mournful rolls
And the mermaid's song condoles, 70
Singing glory to the souls
Of the brave!

THOMAS CAMPBELL.

CHARACTER OF THE HAPPY WARRIOR.

(Nelson died 21 October, 1805)

Who is the happy Warrior? Who is he
Whom every man in arms should wish to be?
It is the generous spirit, who, when brought
Among the tasks of real life, hath wrought
Upon the plan that pleased his childish thought:
Whose high endeavours are an inward light
That make the path before him always bright;
Who, with a natural instinct to discern
What knowledge can perform, is diligent to learn;
Abides by this resolve, and stops not there, 10
But makes his moral being his prime care;

Who, doom'd to go in company with Pain,
And Fear, and Bloodshed, miserable train!
Turns his necessity to glorious gain;
In face of these doth exercise a power
Which is our human nature's highest dower;
Controls them and subdues, transmutes, bereaves
Of their bad influence, and their good receives;
By objects, which might force the soul to abate
Her feeling, render'd more compassionate; 20
Is placable—because occasions rise
So often that demand such sacrifice;
More skilful in self-knowledge, even more pure,
As tempted more; more able to endure
As more exposed to suffering and distress;
Thence, also, more alive to tenderness.
—'Tis he whose law is reason; who depends
Upon that law as on the best of friends!
Whence, in a state where men are tempted still
To evil for a guard against worse ill, 30
And what in quality or act is best
Doth seldom on a right foundation rest,
He fixes good on good alone, and owes
To virtue every triumph that he knows:
Who, if he rise to station of command,
Rises by open means; and there will stand
On honourable terms, or else retire,
And in himself possess his own desire;
Who comprehends his trust, and to the same
Keeps faithful with a singleness of aim; 40
And therefore does not stoop, nor lie in wait
For wealth, or honours, or for worldly state:
Whom they must follow; on whose head must fall,
Like showers of manna, if they come at all:

Whose powers shed round him in the common strife,
Or mild concerns of ordinary life,
A constant influence, a peculiar grace;
But who, if he be call'd upon to face
Some awful moment to which Heaven has join'd
Great issues, good or bad for human kind, 50
Is happy as a lover; and attired
With sudden brightness, like a man inspired:
And through the heat of conflict keeps the law
In calmness made, and sees what he foresaw;
Or if an unexpected call succeed,
Come when it will, is equal to the need:
He who, though thus endued as with a sense
And faculty for storm and turbulence,
Is yet a soul whose master bias leans
To homefelt pleasures and to gentle scenes: 60
Sweet images! which, wheresoe'er he be,
Are at his heart: and such fidelity
It is his darling passion to approve:
More brave for this, that he hath much to love:
'Tis, finally, the man, who, lifted high,
Conspicuous object in a nation's eye,
Or left unthought of in obscurity,—
Who, with a toward or untoward lot,
Prosperous or adverse, to his wish or not,
Plays, in the many games of life, that one, 70
Where what he most doth value must be won;
Whom neither shape of danger can dismay,
Nor thought of tender happiness betray;
Who, not content that former worth stand fast,
Looks forward, persevering to the last,
From well to better, daily self-surpass'd:

Who, whether praise of him must walk the earth
For ever, and to noble deeds give birth,
Or he must go to dust without his fame,
And leave a dead, unprofitable name, 80
Finds comfort in himself and in his cause;
And, while the mortal mist is gathering, draws
His breath in confidence of Heaven's applause:
This is the happy warrior; this is he
Whom every man in arms should wish to be.

WILLIAM WORDSWORTH.

YE MARINERS OF ENGLAND.

(1807)

Ye Mariners of England
  That guard our native seas!
Whose flag has braved a thousand years
  The battle and the breeze!
Your glorious standard launch again
  To match another foe;
And sweep through the deep,
  While the stormy winds do blow!
While the battle rages loud and long,
  And the stormy winds do blow. 10

The spirits of your fathers
  Shall start from every wave—
For the deck it was their field of fame,
  And Ocean was their grave:

Where Blake and mighty Nelson fell
  Your manly hearts shall glow,
As ye sweep through the deep,
  While the stormy winds do blow!
While the battle rages loud and long,
  And the stormy winds do blow. 20

Britannia needs no bulwarks,
  No towers along the steep;
Her march is o'er the mountain-waves,
  Her home is on the deep.
With thunders from her native oak
  She quells the floods below,
As they roar on the shore,
  When the stormy winds do blow!
When the battle rages loud and long,
  And the stormy winds do blow. 30

The meteor flag of England
  Shall yet terrific burn;
Till danger's troubled night depart
  And the star of peace return.
Then, then, ye ocean-warriors!
  Our song and feast shall flow
To the fame of your name,
  When the storm has ceased to blow!
When the fiery fight is heard no more,
  And the storm has ceased to blow. 40

THOMAS CAMPBELL.

THE BURIAL OF SIR JOHN MOORE AT CORUNNA.

(1809)

Not a drum was heard, not a funeral note,
As his corse to the rampart we hurried;
Not a soldier discharged his farewell shot
O'er the grave where our hero we buried.

We buried him darkly, at dead of night,
The sods with our bayonets turning;
By the struggling moonbeam's misty light
And the lanthorn dimly burning.

No useless coffin enclosed his breast,
Not in sheet or in shroud we wound him; 10
But he lay like a warrior taking his rest,
With his martial cloak around him.

Few and short were the prayers we said,
And we spoke not a word of sorrow;
But we steadfastly gazed on the face that was dead,
And we bitterly thought of the morrow.

We thought, as we hollow'd his narrow bed,
And smoothed down his lonely pillow,
That the foe and the stranger would tread o'er his head,
And we far away on the billow! 20

Lightly they'll talk of the spirit that's gone,
And o'er his cold ashes upbraid him,—
But little he'll reck, if they let him sleep on
In the grave where a Briton has laid him.

But half of our heavy task was done
  When the clock struck the note for retiring:
And we heard the distant and random gun
  That the foe was sullenly firing.

Slowly and sadly we laid him down,
  From the field of his fame fresh and gory; 30
We carved not a line, and we raised not a stone,
  But we left him alone with his glory.

CHARLES WOLFE.

WATERLOO.

(from "Childe Harold.")

(1815)

There was a sound of revelry by night,
And Belgium's Capital had gathered then
Her Beauty and her Chivalry—and bright
The lamps shone o'er fair women and brave men;
A thousand hearts beat happily; and when
Music arose with its voluptuous swell,
Soft eyes looked love to eyes which spake again,
And all went merry as a marriage-bell;
But hush! hark! a deep sound strikes like a rising knell!

Did ye not hear it?—No—'twas but the wind, 10
Or the car rattling o'er the stony street;
On with the dance! let joy be unconfined;
No sleep till morn, when Youth and Pleasure meet
To chase the glowing Hours with flying feet—
But hark!—that heavy sound breaks in once more,
As if the clouds its echo would repeat;
And nearer—clearer—deadlier than before!
Arm! Arm! it is—it is—the cannon's opening roar!

Within a windowed niche of that high hall
Sate Brunswick's fated chieftain; he did hear 20
That sound the first amidst the festival,
And caught its tone with Death's prophetic ear;
And when they smiled because he deemed it near,
His heart more truly knew that peal too well
Which stretched his father on a bloody bier,
And roused the vengeance blood alone could quell:
He rushed into the field, and, foremost fighting, fell.

Ah! then and there was hurrying to and fro—
And gathering tears, and tremblings of distress,
And cheeks all pale, which but an hour ago 30
Blushed at the praise of their own loveliness—
And there were sudden partings, such as press
The life from out young hearts, and choking sighs
Which ne'er might be repeated; who could guess
If ever more should meet those mutual eyes,
Since upon night so sweet such awful morn could rise!

And there was mounting in hot haste—the steed,
The mustering squadron, and the clattering car,
Went pouring forward with impetuous speed,
And swiftly forming in the ranks of war— 40
And the deep thunder peal on peal afar;
And near, the beat of the alarming drum
Roused up the soldier ere the Morning Star;
While thronged the citizens with terror dumb,
Or whispering, with white lips—"The foe! They come! they come!"

And wild and high the "Cameron's Gathering" rose!
The war-note of Lochiel, which Albyn's hills
Have heard, and heard, too, have her Saxon foes:—
How in the noon of night that pibroch thrills,
Savage and shrill! But with the breath which fills 50
Their mountain-pipe, so fill the mountaineers
With the fierce native daring which instils
The stirring memory of a thousand years,
And Evan's—Donald's fame rings in each clansman's
ears!

And Ardennes waves above them her green leaves,
Dewy with Nature's tear-drops, as they pass—
Grieving, if aught inanimate e'er grieves,
Over the unreturning brave,—alas!
Ere evening to be trodden like the grass
Which now beneath them, but above shall grow 60
In its next verdure, when this fiery mass
Of living Valour, rolling on the foe,
And burning with high Hope, shall moulder cold and
low.

Last noon beheld them full of lusty life;—
Last eve in Beauty's circle proudly gay;
The Midnight brought the signal-sound of strife,
The Morn the marshalling in arms,—the Day
Battle's magnificently-stern array!
The thunder-clouds close o'er it, which when rent
The earth is covered thick with other clay, 70
Which her own clay shall cover, heaped and pent,
Rider and horse,—friend,—foe,—in one red burial
blent!

Their praise is hymned by loftier hearts than mine;
Yet one I would select from that proud throng,
Partly because they blend me with his line,
And partly that I did his Sire some wrong,
And partly that bright names will hallow song;
And his was of the bravest, and when showered
The death-bolts deadliest the thinned files along,
Even where the thickest of War's tempest lowered, 80
They reached no nobler breast than thine, young, gallant Howard!

There have been tears and breaking hearts for thee,
And mine were nothing, had I such to give;
But when I stood beneath the fresh green tree,
Which living waves where thou didst cease to live,
And saw around me the wide field revive
With fruits and fertile promise, and the Spring
Come forth her work of gladness to contrive,
With all her reckless birds upon the wing,
I turn'd from all she brought to those she could not bring. 90

LORD BYRON.

ENGLAND'S DEAD.

Son of the Ocean Isle!
  Where sleep your mighty dead?
Show me what high and stately pile
  Is reared o'er Glory's bed.

Go, stranger! track the deep—
  Free, free the white sail spread!
Wave may not foam, nor wild wind sweep,
  Where rest not England's dead.

On Egypt's burning plains,
  By the pyramid o'erswayed, 10
With fearful power the noonday reigns,
  And the palm-trees yield no shade;

But let the angry sun
  From heaven look fiercely red,
Unfelt by those whose task is done!—
  There slumber England's dead.

The hurricane hath might
  Along the Indian shore,
And far by Ganges' banks at night
  Is heard the tiger's roar;— 20

But let the sound roll on!
  It hath no tone of dread
For those that from their toils are gone,—
  There slumber England's dead.

Loud rush the torrent-floods
  The Western wilds among,
And free, in green Columbia's woods,
  The hunter's bow is strung;—

But let the floods rush on!
  Let the arrow's flight be sped! 30
Why should they reck whose task is done?—
  There slumber England's dead.

The mountain-storms rise high
  In the snowy Pyrenees,
And toss the pine-boughs through the sky
  Like rose-leaves on the breeze;

But let the storm rage on!
  Let the fresh wreaths be shed!
For the Roncesvalles' field is won,—
  There slumber England's dead. 40

On the frozen deep's repose
  'Tis a dark and dreadful hour,
When round the ship the ice-fields close,
  And the northern night-clouds lour;—

But let the ice drift on!
  Let the cold-blue desert spread!
Their course with mast and flag is done,—
  Even there sleep England's dead.

The warlike of the isles,
  The men of field and wave! 50
Are not the rocks their funeral piles,
  The seas and shores their grave?

Go, stranger! track the deep—
  Free, free the white sail spread
Wave may not foam, nor wild wind sweep
  Where rest not England's dead.

MRS. HEMANS.

VICTORIA'S TEARS.

(1837)

"O maiden! heir of kings!
  A king has left his place!
The majesty of death has swept
  All other from his face!
And thou upon thy mother's breast
  No longer lean adown,
But take the glory for the rest,
And rule the land that loves thee best!"
    She heard, and wept—
  She wept, to wear a crown! 10

  They decked her courtly halls;
  They reined her hundred steeds;
They shouted at her palace gate,
  "A noble Queen succeeds!"
Her name has stirred the mountain's sleep,
  Her praise has filled the town!
And mourners God had stricken deep,
Looked hearkening up, and did not weep.
    Alone she wept,
  Who wept, to wear a crown! 20

She saw no purples shine,
For tears had dimmed her eyes;
She only knew her childhood's flowers
Were happier pageantries!
And while her heralds played the part,
For million shouts to drown—
"God save the Queen" from hill to mart,—
She heard through all her beating heart,
And turned and wept—
She wept, to wear a crown! 30

God save thee, weeping Queen!
Thou shalt be well beloved!
The tyrant's sceptre cannot move
As those pure tears have moved!
The nature in thine eyes we see,
That tyrants cannot own,
The love that guardeth liberties!
Strange blessing on the nation lies,
Whose sovereign wept—
Yea! wept, to wear its crown! 40

God bless thee, weeping Queen,
With blessing more divine!
And fill with happier love than earth's
That tender heart of thine!
That when the thrones of earth shall be
As low as graves brought down,
A piercèd hand may give to thee
The crown which angels shout to see!
Thou wilt not weep,
To wear that heavenly crown! 50

MRS. BROWNING.

ODE ON THE DEATH OF THE DUKE OF WELLINGTON.

(1852)

I.

Bury the Great Duke
With an empire's lamentation,
Let us bury the Great Duke
  To the noise of the mourning of a mighty nation,
Mourning when their leaders fall,
Warriors carry the warrior's pall,
And sorrow darkens hamlet and hall.

II.

Where shall we lay the man whom we deplore?
Here, in streaming London's central roar.
Let the sound of those he wrought for, 10
And the feet of those he fought for,
Echo round his bones for evermore.

III.

Lead out the pageant: sad and slow,
As fits an universal woe,
Let the long long procession go,
And let the sorrowing crowd about it grow,
And let the mournful martial music blow;
The last great Englishman is low.

IV.

Mourn, for to us he seems the last,
Remembering all his greatness in the Past. 20
No more in soldier fashion will he greet
With lifted hand the gazer in the street.
O friends, our chief state-oracle is mute:
Mourn for the man of long-enduring blood,
The statesman-warrior, moderate, resolute,
Whole in himself, a common good.
Mourn for the man of amplest influence,
Yet clearest of ambitious crime,
Our greatest yet with least pretence,
Great in council and great in war, 30
Foremost captain of his time,
Rich in saving common-sense,
And, as the greatest only are,
In his simplicity sublime.
O good gray head which all men knew,
O voice from which their omens all men drew,
O iron nerve to true occasion true,
O fall'n at length that tower of strength
Which stood four-square to all the winds that blew!
Such was he whom we deplore. 40
The long self-sacrifice of life is o'er.
The great World-victor's victor will be seen no more.

V.

All is over and done:
Render thanks to the Giver,
England, for thy son.
Let the bell be toll'd.
Render thanks to the Giver,
And render him to the mould.

Under the cross of gold
That shines over city and river, 50
There he shall rest for ever
Among the wise and the bold.
Let the bell be toll'd:
And a reverent people behold
The towering car, the sable steeds:
Bright let it be with its blazon'd deeds,
Dark in its funeral fold.
Let the bell be toll'd:
And a deeper knell in the heart be knoll'd;
And the sound of the sorrowing anthem roll'd 60
Thro' the dome of the golden cross;
And the volleying cannon thunder his loss;
He knew their voices of old.
For many a time in many a clime
His captain's ear has heard them boom
Bellowing victory, bellowing doom:
When he with those deep voices wrought,
Guarding realms and kings from shame;
With those deep voices our dead captain taught
The tyrant, and asserts his claim 70
In that dread sound to the great name,
Which he has worn so pure of blame,
In praise and in dispraise the same,
A man of well-attemper'd frame.
O civic muse, to such a name,
To such a name for ages long,
To such a name,
Preserve a broad approach of fame,
And ever-echoing avenues of song.

VI.

"Who is he that cometh, like an honour'd guest, 80
With banner and with music, with soldier and with
    priest,
With a nation weeping, and breaking on my rest?"
Mighty Seaman, this is he
Was great by land as thou by sea.
Thine island loves thee well, thou famous man,
The greatest sailor since our world began.
Now, to the roll of muffled drums,
To thee the greatest soldier comes;
For this is he
Was great by land as thou by sea; 90
His foes were thine; he kept us free;
O give him welcome, this is he
Worthy of our gorgeous rites,
And worthy to be laid by thee;
For this is England's greatest son,
He that gain'd a hundred fights,
Nor ever lost an English gun;
This is he that far away
Against the myriads of Assaye
Clash'd with his fiery few and won; 100
And underneath another sun,
Warring on a later day,
Round affrighted Lisbon drew
The treble works, the vast designs
Of his labour'd rampart-lines,
Where he greatly stood at bay,
Whence he issued forth anew,
And ever great and greater grew,

Beating from the wasted vines
Back to France her banded swarms, 110
Back to France with countless blows,
Till o'er the hills her eagles flew
Beyond the Pyrenean pines,
Follow'd up in valley and glen
With blare of bugle, clamour of men,
Roll of cannon and clash of arms,
And England pouring on her foes.
Such a war had such a close.
Again their ravening eagle rose
In anger, wheel'd on Europe-shadowing wings, 120
And barking for the thrones of kings;
Till one that sought but Duty's iron crown
On that loud sabbath shook the spoiler down;
A day of onsets of despair!
Dash'd on every rocky square
Their surging charges foam'd themselves away;
Last, the Prussian trumpet blew;
Thro' the long-tormented air
Heaven flash'd a sudden jubilant ray,
And down we swept and charged and overthrew. 130
So great a soldier taught us there,
What long-enduring hearts could do
In that world-earthquake, Waterloo!
Mighty Seaman, tender and true,
And pure as he from taint of craven guile,
O saviour of the silver-coasted isle,
O shaker of the Baltic and the Nile,
If aught of things that here befall
Touch a spirit among things divine,
If love of country move thee there at all, 140
Be glad, because his bones are laid by thine!

And thro' the centuries let a people's voice
In full acclaim,
A people's voice,
The proof and echo of all human fame,
A people's voice, when they rejoice
At civic revel and pomp and game,
Attest their great commander's claim
With honour, honour, honour, honour to him,
Eternal honour to his name. 150

VII.

A people's voice! we are a people yet.
Tho' all men else their nobler dreams forget,
Confused by brainless mobs and lawless Powers;
Thank Him who isled us here, and roughly set
His Briton in blown seas and storming showers,
We have a voice, with which to pay the debt
Of boundless love and reverence and regret
To those great men who fought, and kept it ours.
And keep it ours, O God, from brute control;
O Statesmen, guard us, guard the eye, the soul 160
Of Europe, keep our noble England whole,
And save the one true seed of freedom sown
Betwixt a people and their ancient throne,
That sober freedom out of which there springs
Our loyal passion for our temperate kings;
For, saving that, ye help to save mankind
Till public wrong be crumbled into dust,
And drill the raw world for the march of mind,
Till crowds at length be sane and crowns be just.
But wink no more in slothful overtrust. 170
Remember him who led your hosts;
He bad you guard the sacred coasts.

Your cannons moulder on the seaward wall;
His voice is silent in your council-hall
For ever; and whatever tempests lour
For ever silent; even if they broke
In thunder, silent: yet remember all
He spoke among you, and the Man who spoke;
Who never sold the truth to serve the hour,
Nor palter'd with Eternal God for power; 180
Who let the turbid streams of rumour flow
Thro' either babbling world of high and low;
Whose life was work, whose language rife
With rugged maxims hewn from life;
Who never spoke against a foe;
Whose eighty winters freeze with one rebuke
All great self-seekers trampling on the right:
Truth-teller was our England's Alfred named;
Truth-lover was our English Duke;
Whatever record leap to light 190
He never shall be shamed.

VIII.

Lo, the leader in these glorious wars
Now to glorious burial slowly borne,
Follow'd by the brave of other lands,
He, on whom from both her open hands
Lavish Honour shower'd all her stars,
And affluent Fortune emptied all her horn.
Yea, let all good things await
Him who cares not to be great,
But as he saves or serves the state. 200
Not once or twice in our rough island-story,
The path of duty was the way to glory:

He that walks it, only thirsting
For the right, and learns to deaden
Love of self, before his journey closes,
He shall find the stubborn thistle bursting
Into glossy purples, which outredden
All voluptuous garden-roses.
Not once or twice in our fair island-story,
The path of duty was the way to glory: 210
He, that ever following her commands,
On with toil of heart and knees and hands,
Thro' the long gorge to the far light has won
His path upward, and prevail'd,
Shall find the toppling crags of Duty scaled
Are close upon the shining table-lands
To which our God Himself is moon and sun.
Such was he: his work is done.
But while the races of mankind endure,
Let his great example stand 220
Colossal, seen of every land,
And keep the soldier firm, the statesman pure:
Till in all lands and thro' all human story
The path of duty be the way to glory:
And let the land whose hearths he saved from shame
For many and many an age proclaim
At civic revel and pomp and game,
And when the long-illumined cities flame,
Their ever-loyal iron leader's fame,
With honour, honour, honour, honour to him, 230
Eternal honour to his name.

IX.

Peace, his triumph will be sung
By some yet unmoulded tongue

Far on in summers that we shall not see:
Peace, it is a day of pain
For one about whose patriarchal knee
Late the little children clung:
O peace, it is a day of pain
For one, upon whose hand and heart and brain
Once the weight and fate of Europe hung. 240
Ours the pain, be his the gain!
More than is of man's degree
Must be with us, watching here
At this, our great solemnity.
Whom we see not we revere;
We revere, and we refrain
From talk of battles loud and vain,
And brawling memories all too free
For such a wise humility
As befits a solemn fane: 250
We revere, and while we hear
The tides of Music's golden sea
Setting toward eternity,
Uplifted high in heart and hope are we,
Until we doubt not that for one so true
There must be other nobler work to do
Than when he fought at Waterloo,
And Victor he must ever be.
For tho' the Giant Ages heave the hill
And break the shore, and evermore 260
Make and break, and work their will;
Tho' world on world in myriad myriads roll
Round us, each with different powers,
And other forms of life than ours,
What know we greater than the soul?

On God and Godlike men we build our trust.
Hush, the Dead March wails in the people's ears:
The dark crowd moves, and there are sobs and tears:
The black earth yawns: the mortal disappears;
Ashes to ashes, dust to dust; 270
He is gone who seem'd so great.—
Gone; but nothing can bereave him
Of the force he made his own
Being here, and we believe him
Something far advanced in State,
And that he wears a truer crown
Than any wreath that man can weave him.
Speak no more of his renown,
Lay your earthly fancies down,
And in the vast cathedral leave him, 280
God accept him, Christ receive him.

LORD TENNYSON.

THE CHARGE OF THE LIGHT BRIGADE.

(1854)

I.

Half a league, half a league,
  Half a league onward,
All in the valley of Death
  Rode the six hundred.
"Forward, the Light Brigade!
Charge for the guns!" he said:
Into the valley of Death
  Rode the six hundred.

II.

"Forward, the Light Brigade!"
Was there a man dismay'd? 10
Not though the soldier knew
  Some one had blunder'd:
Theirs not to make reply,
Theirs not to reason why,
Theirs but to do and die,
Into the valley of Death
  Rode the six hundred.

III.

Cannon to right of them,
Cannon to left of them,
Cannon in front of them 20
  Volley'd and thunder'd;
Storm'd at with shot and shell,
Boldly they rode and well,
Into the jaws of Death,
Into the mouth of Hell
  Rode the six hundred.

IV.

Flash'd all their sabres bare,
Flash'd as they turn'd in air,
Sabring the gunners there,
Charging an army, while 30
  All the world wonder'd:
Plunged in the battery-smoke,
Right through the line they broke;

Cossack and Russian
Reel'd from the sabre-stroke
  Shatter'd and sunder'd.
Then they rode back—but not,
  Not the six hundred.

V.

Cannon to right of them,
Cannon to left of them, 40
Cannon behind them
  Volley'd and thunder'd;
Storm'd at with shot and shell,
While horse and hero fell,
They that had fought so well
Came through the jaws of Death,
Back from the mouth of Hell,
All that was left of them,
  Left of six hundred.

VI.

When can their glory fade? 50
Oh the wild charge they made!
  All the world wonder'd.
Honour the charge they made!
Honour the Light Brigade,
  Noble six hundred!

LORD TENNYSON.

NOTES.

BOADICEA.

Boadicea was queen of the British tribe of the Iceni. In 61, angered by the treatment to which she was subjected by the Romans, she headed a revolt against them. Being defeated, she died, either in battle, or of grief, or by her own hand, according to various accounts.

6. **Druid**, the ancient British priest.

20. **Gaul**: it was the Goths who overthrew the Roman Empire.

31. **eagles**: the Roman standard.

38, 40. **them** refers to 'the bard's prophetic words,' l. 33.

William Cowper (1731—1800) stands in English poetry in a position midway between the artificial school of Pope and the 'return to nature' of which Wordsworth is the type.

KING CANUTE.

On the death of Ethelred in 1016, Canute became king of Northumbria and Mercia, and when Edmund, king of East England and Wessex, died later in the year, Canute was left sole king. The incident recorded in the poem is traditional.

5. **silversticks and goldsticks**: courtiers of a much later date; it is an humorous anachronism.

11. **gleemen**: minstrels.

55. **the Jewish captain**: Joshua. See *Joshua*, x. 13.

William Makepeace Thackeray (1811—1863) was mainly a novelist and satirical writer, and only an occasional poet. This poem is a mock-antique, containing more than one anachronism. It is supposed to be sung by the knight of Ivanhoe in Thackeray's burlesque *Rebecca and Rowena*, a comic continuation and parody of Sir Walter Scott's novel.

HE NEVER SMILED AGAIN.

1. **The bark** was called the White Ship, and the **prince** was William, the only son of Henry I. The ship sank on 25 November, 1120, and tradition records that Henry never smiled afterwards. D. G. Rossetti (1828—1882) wrote a fine ballad *The White Ship* on the same episode.

19. **The tourney**: tournaments or jousts were the sport of knights.

Felicia Dorothea Hemans (1793—1835) during a comparatively short life wrote a great deal of fluent verse of a sentimental kind. Her best-known poem is *Casabianca.*

KING JOHN AND THE ABBOT OF CANTERBURY.

This is a traditional ballad, supposed to be of Oriental origin and a fragment of Coptic folk-lore. A popular story such as this is necessarily of wide vogue, and versions of it appear in Germany in the thirteenth century and in Italy in the fifteenth. It must be understood that when the story came to England, it was fastened upon King John, and does not in fact record an historical incident of that monarch.

19. **dere**: an obsolete word meaning 'harm.'

25. **stead**: position, circumstances.

62. **learn**: this used to mean 'teach,' but now it is only used so vulgarly.

71. **crozier**, an abbot's **staff**: **mitre**, **rochet**, and **cope**, parts of his dress. A **rochet** is a close-fitting surplice.

85. **St. Bittel**, an imaginary saint.

105. nobles, gold coins worth 6*s*. 8*d*.

LAMENT FOR SIMON DE MONTFORT.

Simon de Montfort, Earl of Leicester, was slain at the Battle of Evesham in Worcestershire, 4 August, 1265.

13. The battle was fought on a Tuesday.

31. Sir Hugh le Dispenser, justice of England, killed in the battle.

35. Henry, son of Simon de Montfort.

The English poem was translated by George Ellis (1753—1815), a satirical verse-writer and contributor to the *Anti-Jacobin*, from an early poem in French, evidently written by one of Simon de Montfort's adherents.

ROBIN HOOD AND THE THREE SQUIRES.

Robin Hood is not historical, but a popular hero created by ballads. No reference to him is known earlier than the end of the fourteenth century, but he was doubtless a popular character before that date. The best ballads of Robin Hood belong to the fifteenth century; but the present one is obviously of later workmanship, compiled in the seventeenth century by some hack-writer. None the less, it is typical of the courteous and free outlaw, who throughout is representative of the yeoman as opposed to the higher orders, spiritual and temporal, upon whom he levies toll. Traditionally, he is associated with Nottingham, as in this ballad, and with Barnsdale in the West Riding of Yorkshire, between Barnsley, Doncaster, Wakefield, and Pontefract.

19. **palmer**, pilgrim.

52. **list**, desire, wish.

62. Probably a corruption of 'May Heaven you save and see,' see being an old word meaning 'protect.'

96. **shining**, a corruption of some word equivalent to 'hastening'; perhaps 'skimming.'

101. **slack**, a pass between two hills.

BOLD ROBIN.

The poem illustrates Robin Hood's traditional method of dealing with the friars.

1. **ghostly**, spiritual, priestly.

35. **angels**, gold coins of value varying between a third and a half of a pound.

Thomas Love Peacock (1785—1866), a friend of Shelley, was a novelist, satirist, and poet, whose novels undoubtedly influenced Thackeray. *Bold Robin* comes in the novel *Maid Marian*, and is one of the best of Peacock's songs, most of which attain a very high standard.

DURHAM FIELD.

This battle was fought on October 17, 1346, but the ballad was not written till at least 130 years later, and some of the minstrel's statements are not in accordance with any of the accounts of the battle. Edward III being in France at the siege of Calais, David Bruce, the young king of Scotland, took the opportunity to invade England, and was met at Durham by an English force in three divisions, one (says the English chronicle) under the Earl of Angus, Henry Percy, Ralph Neville, and Henry Scrope, the second under the Archbishop of York, and the third under Mowbray, Rokeby, and John of Copland. The Scots' three divisions, according to the Scottish chronicle, were led (i) by King David Bruce, (ii) the Earl of Murray and William Douglas, and (iii) the Steward of Scotland and the Earl of March.

2. **spell**, while.

8. **busked**, prepared themselves: **boun**, ready. The whole phrase constantly occurs in ballads. See l. 102, 150.

12. **stound**, time.

23. **leeve**, dear, pleasant: a common epithet of London.

32. **bearen**: an old plural form; cf. ll. 128, 192, 193.

37. **Hard hansel**, bad omen.

40. **For**, for fear of.

41. **Anguish** = Angus. The minstrel absurdly puts him with the Scots.

49. **Vaughan** is probably Buchan.

55. **vanward**, vanguard, front of battle.

65. **Neville** was also on the English side.

74. **breme**, fierce.

79. **Marches**, the Border.

93. **Westchester**, Chester.

105. The minstrel is wrong again.

109. **But all only**, all except.

158. **ancients**, ensigns, flags.

163. **Fluwilliams** is probably meant to represent Llewellyn, a name which Shakespeare spells Fluellen; but the lord is unknown.

173. **orders**, prepares.

180. **may**, maiden; the Virgin Mary.

184. **scantly**, scarcely.

192, 193. See note on l. 32.

196. **dree**, endure, hold out.

199. Notice **thorough** in this line and the next, an old form of *through* surviving in *thoroughfare*.

241. **food**, man, knight.

247. **leve**, grant.

253—6. A grotesque error of the minstrel. Creçy was fought 26 August, 1346, and Poictiers on 19 September, 1356.

CHEVY CHASE.

This is a seventeenth-century version of an older ballad, *The Hunting of the Cheviot*, which is apparently founded upon the story of the Battle of Otterburn, fought 19 August, 1388. All that is left in the present ballad is a duel between Earl Percy of Northumberland and Earl Douglas. This version was appraised by Joseph Addison (1672—1719) in the *Spectator*; while Sir Philip Sidney's eulogy of an earlier version is even more famous.

4. **Chevy**, Cheviot; **Chase**, hunting-ground.

37. **quarry**, deer killed in the hunt.

49. **Tividale**, Teviotdale, in the south of Scotland near the Border. A tributary of the **Tweed** flows through it.

58. **But and if**: 'and if' is equivalent to 'if,' while 'but' goes with 'I durst encounter.' The meaning is, 'There was never yet a champion whom I dared not encounter, if it so fell out.'

106. **bade**, abode, waited; **bent**, field, grass.

119. **wood**, mad; **laid on load**, dealt heavy blows.

143. **Forwhy**: an old English word meaning *because*. Cf. in the 'Old Hundredth' hymn (nearly always wrongly printed as two words, and with a mark of interrogation):

"Forwhy the Lord our God is good."

198 ff. These names vary in the different versions, and their owners for the most part cannot be identified with any certainty.

242. **Humbledown**, the battle of Homildon Hill, near Wooler in Northumberland, fought 1402, in which Henry IV defeated the Scots; but the ballad is again out, as James (l. 225) was not crowned till 1424.

THE BATTLE OF HARLAW.

This battle was fought on 24 July, 1411, between Donald of the Isles and an army of Lowlanders under the Earl of Mar and the sheriff of Angus. Donald, whom the ballad calls "Macdonell," laid claim to the Earldom of Ross, and was advancing on Aberdeen when he was met at Harlaw and defeated. He lost 900 men, and the victors 500.

1—4. **I**: the ballad is put into the mouth of 'John Hielan'man,' who meets two knights, both unknown to history. **Dunidier** is a hill on the Aberdeen road near **Harlaw**, which is 18 miles N.W. of Aberdeen. **Netherhall** is close by.

7. **Balquhain** is a mile south of Harlaw.

16. **she** means 'I.' In Scottish dialect one might have expected 'her.'

26. **Gin**, if.

27. **meikle** = mickle, much.

31. **maun**, must.

33. We'll try what we can do.

43. **sair**, sore. So **mair** in l. 45 = more.

49. **we'se**, we shall.

60. **Drumminnor**: more than twenty miles away, but the horse covers the distance there and back in two hours and a quarter!

61. **fess**, fetch.

74. **ae**, one, single.

78. **lierachie**, hubbub, confusion. Pronounce as four syllables.

90—93. This, of course, must be largely discounted.

98. **speer at**, ask of. See *Dick o' the Cow*, 57, note.

THE AGINCOURT SONG.

This and the two following pieces relate to Henry V's expedition into France in 1415, when he captured Harfleur and won the battle of Agincourt (25 October).

This is a contemporary song, written when the sword was mightier than the pen. It is here reduced to modern English; and must be read so as to bring out the final rimes.

1. Henry landed at the mouth of the Seine; cf. Drayton's poem, l. 6.

5, 6. The Latin *refrain* means:—"England, render thanks to God for the victory."

7. **the sooth for to say**, to tell the truth. Perhaps the should be *thee*, meaning 'to tell *you* the truth.'

14. **Frenchë**: a form of the genitive.

15. In modern English we should insert 'neither' before the word 'for.'

16. **Agincourt** is about half-way between the river Somme and Calais.

32. **well-willing**, well-wishers, adherents.

KING HENRY THE FIFTH'S CONQUEST OF FRANCE.

The story of the tennis-balls is scarcely to be accepted as historical, though it is supported by tradition from contemporary chronicles. Shakespeare made use of it in his play of *Henry V* (Act I, Scene 2).

14. **he**: bad grammar necessitated by the rime.

19. Some accounts say it was a 'ton' of tennis-balls.

35—6. There is no historical confirmation of this kindness on Henry's part.

49. This also lacks authority. Henry left France as soon as possible after the battle.

55—6. This refers to the subsequent marriage of Henry V to Katharine, the daughter of Charles VI of France.

AGINCOURT.

This poem, written two centuries after the battle, is a more circumstantial account of the incident than either of the foregoing pieces.

3. **prove**, try, make trial of.

6. **Caux** was where Havre now stands.

13—16. The French army took up their position at Agincourt, barring the way to Calais, whither Henry V was marching.

17. **Which** refers to the French general.

19. **his** refers to Henry, and so does he in l. 21.

24. **their** refers to the French, the 'nation vile.' Notice the bad construction of this verse; the grammar is involved.

27. **As a** matter of fact the French were about four or five times the number of the English, who were eight or ten thousand strong.

41. **Poictiers** (1356) was partially, and **Creçy** (1346) mainly, won by English archers; therefore 'swords' is misleading.

49. **The Duke of York**: grandson of Edward III.

50. **vaward**=vanguard; see note on *Durham Field*, l. 55.

53. **Excester**: old spelling of Exeter. John Holland, afterwards Duke of Exeter, was in the battle, but the rear was led by Lord Camoys.

66. Sir Thomas **Erpingham** was marshal of the English army.

82. **bilbos**, swords, from Bilbao in Spain.

89. **This while**, meanwhile.

91. **ding**, hurl.

93. **lent**, gave.

94. **besprent**, sprinkled.

97. Humphrey Duke of **Gloucester**, the king's youngest brother.

101. The Duke of **Clarence**, Henry's third brother, was not at the battle. Nor was the Earl of Warwick (l. 105).

113. **Saint Crispin's Day**, October 25, is the feast of two saints, Crispin and Crispinian. The battle of Balaclava took place on the same day in 1854.

Michael Drayton (?1563—1631) was a Jacobean poet who compiled many long poems, historical and topographical. He wrote a longer poem also on Agincourt, but this, and one of his sonnets, are the best-known pieces.

THE ROSE OF ENGLAND.

This poem is remarkable amongst traditional ballads for having an allegory, sustained almost throughout. It deals with the winning of the crown of England from Richard III by the Earl of Richmond, afterwards Henry VII.

1. The **garden** is, of course, England.

7. **the rose so red**, Henry VI. A red rose was the badge of the house of Lancaster.

8. **rise**, twig, branch.

13. The **boar** stands for Richard III, whose cognisance was a boar argent.

15. **the seed of the rose**, Richmond.

17. Richard was supposed to have murdered Henry VI and his son Edward.

21. The eagle is Lord Stanley, afterwards Earl of Derby, whose castle was at Lathom. It is not an historical fact that he was protector of Richmond.

26. lain, conceal.

31. A blue boar was the cognisance of the Earl of Oxford.

32. the boar so white; see l. 13 and note.

49. wend, go.

52. at his own lust, as he desires.

56. shogged them, moved themselves.

57. baily, bailiff. Cf. l. 72.

63. The ballad-maker has recorded only part of a humorous incident. Mitton had sworn to admit no enemy of King Richard to the town except over his own body, meaning that he would die in defence of the town. Richmond proposed, therefore, that Mitton should lie down, and he would step over his body; and this ('I am sure the chronicles will not lie') was actually done!

75. head, behead.

93. Atherstone, near Bosworth Field.

97. The bird was Lord Strange, son of Stanley.

101. verament, truly.

105. vanward: see note on *Durham Field*, l. 55.

111. A talbot (a kind of dog) was the badge of the Talbot family, Earls of Shrewsbury. This one was Sir Gilbert Talbot.

112. The unicorn stands for Sir John Savage. did him quite, acquitted himself.

113. the hart's head, Sir William Stanley, Lord Stanley's brother.

SIR ANDREW BARTON.

This splendid and amusing ballad is founded on an historical incident of the reign of Henry VIII. The Portuguese had seized a ship commanded by Sir Andrew Barton's father, and the son was therefore given letters of reprisal from the King of Scotland. He seems to have abused this privilege, and in 1511 Sir Thomas and Sir Edward Howard were sent by Henry VIII to capture him. Sir Andrew Barton was killed and his ship, the *Lion*, was taken.

18. **mickle**, much, great. See *The Battle of Harlaw*, l. 27.

29. The ballad-maker has got the name wrong; see above.

48. **thou'st**=thou shalt. Cf. ll. 244, 309; and see *The Battle of Harlaw*, l. 49, and note.

52. **bread**, breadth. The line means 'if I miss my aim by the breadth of three pennies.' Cf. l. 64.

91. **archboard**. It is not known exactly what is meant by this word, here or in l. 114, but the meaning is clear. Perhaps it is the same as 'hatch-board' in ll. 141, 278. Here the sense is 'he grappled my ship to the side of his.'

99. **thee fro**=from thee.

104. **wot**, understand, know.

109. **dearly dight**, handsomely fitted out.

114. The meaning of this line is not clear. See above, l. 91.

116. **And if**=if, even if; cf. l. 136.

134. **taken me sworn**, exacted an oath of me, *i.e.* liberated me on parole.

140. After this verse there is a dramatic interval of a night.

142. See l. 109.

145. **ancients**, ensigns. See *Durham Field*, l. 158.

152. **can**, know; here it means 'practise,' or 'show.'

155. **Portingale**, Portuguese.

172. **moe**: an old form of 'more.'

182. **that**: a superfluous word often occurring in these ballads; cf. ll. 214, 226.

186. **Weet**=wit [ye], know.

208. The **beams** appear to have been an engine of naval warfare, perhaps for grappling two ships together, like the ancient *corvus*. See l. 116, and later l. 220.

209. **swarved**, swarmed, climbed.

211. **a bearing arrow** was perhaps an extra long arrow, or a light arrow for long-distance shooting. But cf. l. 223.

227—8. This is the ballad-maker's comment.

248. **ship** is perhaps a mistake for 'scrip,' bag, or quiver.

251. **spole**=Scottish 'spauld,' shoulder.

255. **jack**, coat of mail.

266. **lay**, wager, bet.

272. **the rest** [who] **were**: for this omission of the relative, cf. l. 275.

280. **thou lands**=thou landest. Cf. l. 74.

293. **he** means the King.

300. This astonishing remark is the ballad-maker's own invention.

310. **store**, plenty.

317. *i.e.* went into another room.

FLODDEN FIELD.

The battle of Flodden was fought 9 September, 1513, between James IV of Scotland and an English force under the Earl of Surrey. Flodden is near the Scottish border in Northumberland. The Scots were beaten, and James killed.

8. **lovely**: cf. 'leeve London' in *Durham Field*, l. 23, and note.

9. **Margaret** was the sister of Henry VIII, who was absent in France. Her remonstrance with her husband is an historical fact.

21. **Lord Thomas Howard** was the Earl of Surrey. He had conducted Margaret to Scotland for her marriage in 1503; which is sufficient ground for the ballad-maker to introduce him as her chamberlain ten years later.

26. **mome**, fool, dolt.

29 and 31. **Flodden** is the name of the hill; **Bramstone**, now Brankston, is a village hard by.

37. The Scots lost certainly 10,000 men, including members of nearly all their aristocratic families.

45. **Jack with a feather** is a contemptuous phrase directed at James IV's foolhardiness. **lapt all in leather**: bodies were sometimes wrapped in leather first, and then in lead, or *vice versa*.

47. **morrice-dance**: an old-fashioned festival dance.

EDINBURGH AFTER FLODDEN.

This poem gives the Scottish aspect of the battle, showing the receipt of the news of defeat.

15. This was a popular superstition of old.

51. **riven**, torn.

113. **Dunedin**, Edinburgh.

166. **Southron**: a Scottish term for Englishmen, living south of the border.

225. **leaguer**, camp: the same word as the Dutch 'laager.'

William Edmonstoune Aytoun (1813—1865) was part-author of the *Bon Gaultier Ballads*, an admirable book of light verse, and author of *Lays of the Scottish Cavaliers*, whence this poem and *The Burial March of Dundee* (p. 141) are taken.

DICK O' THE COW.

This traditional ballad is representative of a number of fine heroic ballads of the Border between England and Scotland, many centring round Liddesdale, a long valley running north-east from above Carlisle and containing the Liddel river. The Armstrong family in particular were notorious cattle-raiders and freebooters, and Johnnie has a ballad to himself.

The 'Cow' in 'Dickie's' name does not refer to cattle, as the Scottish form of that is 'ky.' 'Cow' probably means 'brush' or 'broom': see l. 35.

2. **riding** means riding out to steal cattle, or raiding.

3. **lidder**, lazy.

6. **Billie** is not a proper name here: 'billie' is Scottish for brother, and it is the same word as 'bully,' used by Shakespeare of Bottom the weaver in *A Midsummer Night's Dream*. Cf. l. 74.

7. **feed**, feud.

18. **know**, knoll, hill.

31. **he**, of course, is Dick o' the Cow.

32. *i.e.* cease your crying.

52. **sta'**=stole.

54. **Hairibee**, the place of execution in Carlisle.

57. **at**=from: so constantly with verbs of asking.

61. **Puddinburn** is said to have been a house in the middle of Liddesdale.

62. **dree**, endure, hold out.

81. **his burden of batts**, all the blows he can bear. This verse has an extra line in it for some reason.

85. **hough**=hock, heel.

87. **dought**, was able.

93. **mense**, pen, house.

95. **Mangertoun** is another house in Liddesdale.

98. **aevery**, ravenous.

104. **St. Mary knot**, a triple knot.

130. **jack**, jerkin. Cf. *Sir Andrew Barton*, l. 255.

131. **hang leugh**, hung low.

137. **Cannobie** is near the lower end of Liddesdale.

141. **mo**, old form of 'more.' Cf. *Sir Andrew Barton*, l. 172.

143. **lee-lang**, livelong; the whole (day).

158. **blan**, stopped.

161. **plummet**, pommel.

164. **Gramercie** = *grand merci*, great thanks.

186. **gart** = garred, made, caused.

187. **limmer**, rascal.

224. **and** = if. Cf. l. 241, and often elsewhere.

238. **lap a loup**, leapt a leap.

239. **leugh**, laughed.

EARL BOTHWELL.

The ballad-maker, obviously a supporter of Darnley, represents that the 'king' (Darnley) was murdered by way of revenge for his participation in the murder of David Riccio, the Queen's favourite, here called 'Lord David.' He also says that Mary sent for Darnley to come to Scotland, and that she was 'bitterly banished' by the Regent Murray. The ballad therefore cannot be taken as historically accurate.

1. **Woe worth thee** = woe be to thee.

2. **sleight**, trick.

10. *i.e.* to be above lords.

12. This is a proverb, signifying that privileges have their drawbacks, or that one has to pay the price of exalted rank.

19. **And tho'** = even though.

24. Some accounts say that Riccio received fifty wounds.

30. **rushes** were formerly strewn on floors in place of carpets.

33. **boun**, ready. Cf. *Durham Field*, l. 8.

37. **lope**, leapt.

39. **Bothwell**: James Hepburn, Earl of Bothwell, Queen Mary's second husband, either himself slew Darnley, or ordered him to be slain, as he was trying to escape after the explosion of gunpowder from a house called Kirk o' Field, near Edinburgh. How far Mary was privy to the plot is disputed; but certainly she married Bothwell shortly afterwards.

50. **deemedst**: *deem* is an older form of *doom*.

THE RISING IN THE NORTH.

This ballad gives only an imperfect account of the rebellion in 1569 of the Earls of Northumberland and Westmoreland, with Richard Norton, sheriff of York, and others, in support of Mary, then in prison at Tutbury, and in opposition to Queen Elizabeth. On 14 November, they entered Durham Cathedral, tore up the English Bible and Prayer-book, and said mass. A month later they were met at Wetherby by an English army under the Earls of Warwick and Clinton, and fled without fighting.

1, 2. This is a characteristic opening of old ballads and romances. **Lithe**, attend.

28. **borrow**, hostage, security.

44. **blan**: from *blin*, to linger. Cf. l. 136, and *Dick o' the Cow*, l. 158.

51. **I wis**: the old English *i-wis*=surely, was later on confused with *I wiss*, a mistaken form of *I wot*=I know.

59. **hight**, promised.

61. **Gramercy**=*grand merci*, great thanks. Cf. *Dick o' the Cow*, l. 164.

65. Richard Norton had eleven sons, seven of whom engaged in the rebellion, and eight daughters. Francis, the eldest son, as a matter of fact took a prominent part, though Christopher was the most ardent. It was rather William who refused to rebel.

89. **wend**, go.

92. **dee**: northern form of die.

93. Norton was seventy-one years of age at the time.

101. **ancient**, ensign: see *Durham Field*, l. 158.

103. One greyhound's head appears on the Nevilles' banner, with a dun bull.

114. Sir George Bowes surrendered Barnard Castle on 12 December.

121. **leeve**: see note on *Durham Field*, l. 23.

136. **stint**, stopped: **blan**, see l. 44.

146. **ruth**, pity.

MARY AMBREE.

There is no historical foundation known for this exploit, which is supposed to have taken place at the siege of Ghent in 1584. The ballad became very popular, and Ben Jonson constantly refers to it. Rudyard Kipling has taken the title of one of his books from the first line.

2. **Gaunt**, Ghent, in Flanders.

5. **Sir John Major** is unknown. Possibly the words are a corruption of 'sergeant-major.'

BRAVE LORD WILLOUGHBY.

It is impossible to say with certainty to what 'fight' this song refers, but it may perhaps refer to the battle of Zutphen, where Sir Philip Sidney lost his life, in 1586. Lord Willoughby died in 1601.

8. **Lord Willoughby** was Peregrine Bertie, who inherited the title of Baron Willoughby of Eresby from his mother.

9. Sir John **Norris**, by whose side Lord Willoughby fought in several engagements in the Netherlands.

11. **Turner** was also a well-known soldier in the Low Countries.

21. **caliver**, gun.

38. **savourly**, with good appetite.

55. **stout**, bold.

THE ARMADA.

5. The exact date was 30 July.

7. **Aurigny's isle**; the French name for Alderney, one of the Channel Islands.

12. **Edgecumbe**: Mount Edgecumbe is west of Plymouth Sound.

14. **post**, messenger.

16. **halberdiers**, men carrying a long-handled axe.

21—2. A description of the English standard; **the gay lilies** are the lilies of France.

23. **Picard field**, Creçy. The next line refers to John of Bohemia, the Genoese crossbow-men, and Charles, afterwards Emperor.

30. **semper eadem** (=always the same) was Queen Elizabeth's motto.

35. Eddystone, a rock now bearing a famous and important light-house, off Plymouth; **Berwick** on the Scotch border; **Lynn,** King's Lynn in Norfolk; **Milford Bay** in South Wales.

38. **Saint Michael's Mount** in Cornwall; **Beachy Head** in Sussex.

41. The chain of signal-fires proceeds from Devon and Somerset (Longleat is near Frome) to Wiltshire, Dorsetshire, and Hampshire.

46. There is a gap in the chain here, as Richmond could not see beacons either at Clifton or Beaulieu.

65. **Darwin** probably means the Derwent in the Peak District of Derbyshire.

71. **Belvoir,** the seat of the Duke of Rutland, on the borders of Lincolnshire and Leicestershire.

73. **Gaunt's embattled pile,** Lancaster Castle, rebuilt by John of Gaunt, Duke of Lancaster.

Thomas Babington, Lord Macaulay (1800—1859) was chiefly an historian and politician, and the bulk of his verse is not large. This splendid fragment, which was no doubt an experiment suggested by a similar description of a chain of beacons in the *Agamemnon* of Aeschylus, illustrates his mastery of the use of proper names.

THE DEFEAT OF THE SPANISH ARMADA.

This is a seventeenth-century song illustrative of the general rejoicings caused by the defeat of the Armada. It was sung to the tune of 'Jog on, jog on,' a verse of which is sung by Autolycus in Shakespeare's *Winter's Tale*, Act IV, Scene 2.

3. The Armada left Lisbon at the end of May.

7. **bravado,** boast.

13. **Don Pedro** means the Duke of Medina Sidonia.

14. **the Knight of the Sun** was the hero of an old romantic tale, translated from Spanish.

48. **speed,** fare, suffer.

THE FAME OF SIR FRANCIS DRAKE.

This little contemporary poem is included for the sake of the quaint suggestion in the last couplet. Drake began his famous voyage of circumnavigation in 1577, and travelling from east to west, like the sun, arrived home in 1580. The sun therefore overtook and passed 'his fellow-traveller' more than a thousand times!

CAPTAIN WARD AND THE *RAINBOW*.

Captain John Ward was a 'rover' or pirate from about 1604—1609. The *Rainbow* was the name of one of the ships taken by Drake in the expedition to Cadiz in 1587. The incidents in the ballad lack authority.

89—93. The king regrets the loss of George **Clifford**, Earl of Cumberland; Charles Blount, Lord **Mountjoy**; and Robert Devereux, Earl of **Essex**, already referred to in l. 71.

WHEN THE KING ENJOYS HIS OWN AGAIN.

A famous Jacobite song, sung to a still more famous tune (which was also used by Hanoverians in later years), it first supported the interests of Charles I, then encouraged the Cavaliers, promoted the Restoration of Charles II, and after 1688 was the mainstay of the adherents of the exiled family.

1. **Booker**, with **Pond**, **Rivers**, **Swallow**, **Dove**, and **Dade** below, were astrologers and makers of almanacs containing prophecies for the year.

31. This line dates the song to 1643.

Martin Parker was one of the most prominent ballad-writers of the seventeenth century, who got their living by writing verses, on popular subjects, printed as 'broadsides' and hawked about the streets. Very little is known of his life.

SIR NICHOLAS AT MARSTON MOOR.

The battle was fought 2 July, 1644, Prince Rupert and Newcastle leading the Royalist army against a larger one under Cromwell, who won a decisive victory.

3. **Lucas**; Sir Charles Lucas led a division of Royalists.

15. **Fairfax** held the right wing of Cromwell's army, both foot and horse.

21. Cf. *The Battle of Naseby*, l. 12.

52. William **Lenthall** was Speaker of the House of Commons. Hugh **Peters** was an army-chaplain and preacher.

Winthrop Mackworth Praed (1802—1839) was a writer of graceful and charming verse in various styles.

THE BATTLE OF NASEBY.

Naseby, fought 14 June, 1645, was the final defeat of Charles I, and another success for Cromwell and his son-in-law Ireton.

11. **The Man of Blood**, Charles I.

12. **Astley** and **Sir Marmaduke** Langdale were in command of bodies of cavalry.

25. Rupert's charge broke the left wing of the Parliamentary army under Ireton, but the Prince went too far in pursuit, as he had done at Edge Hill.

29. **Skippon** led the infantry in the centre of Cromwell's army, and was hard pressed; but Cromwell came to his assistance from the right wing.

43. **broad-pieces**, money.

46. **lemans**, an old English word for sweethearts.

57. **she of the seven hills**: Rome, built on seven hills.

ON THE LORD GENERAL FAIRFAX AT THE SIEGE OF COLCHESTER.

Sir Thomas Fairfax was the general-in-chief of the Parliamentary army, and when the Royalists attempted further risings, two years after the overthrow of Charles I, Fairfax laid siege to Colchester and took it, 28 August, 1648, thus ending the most important of such disturbances.

3. This is exaggerated praise, though Fairfax was very successful.

7. **Hydra**: one of the labours of Hercules was to slay the Hydra, a monster with a hundred heads, whose quality was such that two more sprang up for each one cut off. Cf. *The Fire of London*, l. 93.

8. **imp**: a term used in falconry to mean the mending of a bird's wing artificially.

13. **fraud**: a reference to the suspected misappropriation of public moneys by a section of the Parliamentarians.

John Milton (1608—1674), England's second greatest poet, wrote very little of his poetry during the twenty years of civil war and disturbance, but a great deal of controversial matter in beautiful if faulty prose.

AN HORATIAN ODE UPON CROMWELL'S RETURN FROM IRELAND.

This ode is called Horatian on account of the resemblance of its literary form to the odes of Horace. Cromwell returned from Ireland in May, 1650.

4. **numbers**, verses. Cf. 'I am ill at these numbers,' *Hamlet*, II. 2; and Longfellow's *Psalm of Life*, 'Tell me not in mournful numbers.'

15. **thorough**: see note on *Durham Field*, l. 199.

18. **emulous**, jealous.

23. **Caesar** means the King.

32. **bergamot**, a kind of pear-tree.

46. *i.e.* where did not Cromwell inflict the heaviest blow?

47. **Hampton** refers to the King's stay at Hampton Court during 1647, whence he fled to the Isle of Wight and became a prisoner in Carisbrook Castle.

66. **assured**, made secure.

67—72. This refers to a legend of ancient Rome. When the foundations were being dug for a temple on the Capitol, the workmen, it was said, saw a human head, which was supposed to be prophetic of the future success of the city.

79. The Irish did not consider Cromwell's treatment 'just,' or even justifiable.

87. **what he may**, as far as he can.

104. **climacteric** here means dangerous, or critical. Derived from the Greek word for a 'step' in a ladder, it originally meant *periodical*; and thence it was applied to recurrent diseases, or periods of life which were supposed to be dangerous.

105. **Pict**: the early inhabitants of Scotland were so called.

Andrew Marvell (1621—1678), member of Parliament for Hull, a friend of Milton, and an admirer of Cromwell, wrote most of his poetry in the first half of his life. Later he became an ardent politician, and wrote violent satire.

TO CROMWELL.

Milton addressed this sonnet to Cromwell in the year after the 'crowning mercy' of his victory at Worcester, 3 September, 1651, and the year before the end of the Long Parliament, 1653.

7. **Darwen**: a stream flowing into the Ribble in Lancashire, near which the invading Scots under the Duke of Hamilton had been routed in 1648, in the battle of Preston.

8. **Dunbar**, near North Berwick, was the scene of another victory of Cromwell's in 1650.

12. The emphasised word is **souls**. Milton hints to Cromwell that after his conquests under arms he must enter into religious conflict with the intolerant Presbyterians, whom Milton calls 'hireling wolves.'

THE FIRE OF LONDON.

This calamity took place in September, 1666, the fire burning for three days.

2. **France and Holland**: the struggle with the Dutch, due to commercial rivalry, had been going on for five years when in 1665 they called on Louis XIV of France to assist them. Engagements took place off the mouth of the Thames, in which the English were eventually successful.

22. It began in a baker's shop, in Pudding Lane, near New Fish Street.

23. All the City from the Tower to Temple Bar was destroyed, including old St Paul's Cathedral.

45. **letted**, hindered.

49. Traitors' heads, after execution, were fixed on London Bridge.

74. **The fate of Simois**: Simois is a mistake for Xanthus or Scamander, a river that was dried up by Hephaestus for trying to drown Achilles. See Homer's *Iliad*, Book xxi.

101. The fire began to abate on the evening of the 5th of September.

114. The fire was undoubtedly beneficial in the event to the city of London; and the subsequent widening of the streets helped to banish the dreaded Plague from England.

John Dryden (1631—1700), poet laureate 1670—1700, was both poet, dramatist, and critic. As poet and essayist he stands head and shoulders above his contemporaries, and very high in English literature; but his plays are not so distinguished. This piece is extracted from a longer poem called *Annus Mirabilis*, a history in verse of the eventful year 1666.

THE SONG OF THE WESTERN MEN.

Lines 6—8 of this poem have been proverbial in Cornwall ever since James II in 1688 imprisoned the Seven Bishops, one of whom was Sir Jonathan Trelawney.

11. **Michael's hold**, Saint Michael's Mount, in Cornwall (see *The Armada*, l. 38).

13. **Tamar**, the river dividing Cornwall from Devonshire (see *The Armada*, l. 41).

Robert Stephen Hawker (1803—1875) wrote several volumes of verse. This poem, based on three traditional lines (see above), was first printed anonymously in a newspaper, which led to its being taken for the original traditional poem; and as such it deceived Sir Walter Scott, Lord Macaulay, and Charles Dickens who all praised it. Hawker wrote it in 1825.

THE BURIAL MARCH OF DUNDEE.

John Graham (or Graeme), formerly Claverhouse and then Viscount Dundee, gathered the Highland clans round him and rose against William and Mary and on behalf of James II, in 1689. He was met by William's general, Mackay, in the Pass of Killiecrankie, on 27 July; and the Highlanders from a commanding position swept the English down the pass.

24. **Montrose**, another Graham, the first to discover the capacity of the Highlanders for war.

28. **Schehallion**, the mountain overlooking the Pass of Killiecrankie.

36. On 3 May, 1679, the Archbishop of St Andrews was murdered by Covenanters on **Magus Muir**, near St Andrews.

91. **slogan**, war-cry.

ADMIRAL BENBOW.

1. Admiral John Benbow (1653—1702) was cruising in the West Indies, not **Virginia** nor **Fayal** (which is in the Azores), when on 19 August he sighted a French squadron.

3. The English ships were seven in number, the French nine, of which four were men-of-war, one a transport, and four small frigates.

13. The engagement lasted from 21 August to the 24th, the morning on which Benbow's right leg was shattered by a chain-shot.

19. Benbow, on the contrary, insisted on being carried up, after his wound was dressed, to the quarter-deck.

23. Benbow died at Port Royal and was buried at Kingston, in Jamaica, in November, 1702.

AFTER BLENHEIM.

This poem is a satire both on the horrors of war in general, and on the far-reaching causes of this battle in particular, which was the greatest in the war of the Spanish Succession. The English under the Duke of Marlborough, with their Austrian allies under Prince Eugene, defeated the French and Bavarians at Blenheim in 1704.

23. The English and their allies lost 5000 men, and the French many more.

Robert Southey (1774—1843), poet laureate from 1813—1843, was during his life associated with Coleridge and Wordsworth, who succeeded him in the laureateship; but he is now under-rated. Other well-known poems of his are *How the water comes down at Lodore, The Inchcape Rock*, and *Bishop Hatto.*

THE VICAR OF BRAY.

A certain Canon of Windsor is said to have been Vicar of Bray, near Maidenhead, from 1540 to 1588, and to have been a Papist under Henry VIII, a Protestant under Edward VI, a Papist again under Mary, and a Protestant again under Elizabeth. This gave rise to a proverb, 'The Vicar of Bray will be Vicar of Bray still.' This song, which is said to have been written by a soldier in the reign of George I, does not record history so much as illustrate the continued change of religious and political opinion in England from the time of the Stuarts to the Hanoverians.

A BALLAD OF THE BOSTON TEA-PARTY.

In 1770 Lord North caused Parliament to abolish all duties except that on tea, which he acknowledged he retained to assert England's right to tax the Colonies. In 1773, a large quantity of tea arrived in

Boston Harbour, and some of the inhabitants disguised themselves as Red Indians, and flung the whole of the tea overboard.

63. The **Dartmouth** was one of the tea-ships.

82. **rock**, distaff (a Scottish word).

104. **Hyson**, the name of a once-familiar brand of tea. See *The Ingoldsby Legends*:

> But I and my son
> Mix black with our Hyson.

THE LOSS OF THE *ROYAL GEORGE*.

The *Royal George* of 108 guns sank in the Solent off Spithead in 1782.

5. The number drowned was over 900.

7, 8. The ship was 'careened,' or laid on one side, for repairs.

22. Admiral Kempenfelt was writing in his cabin at the moment of the disaster.

30. The ship was never raised.

THE BATTLE OF THE BALTIC.

In 1801 England sent a fleet under Admiral Sir Hyde Parker, with Nelson second in command, into the Baltic to intimidate the alliance known as the Armed Neutrality, one of whose objects was the diminution of the English domination of the sea. The fleet first demanded that the Danes should leave the Alliance, and on their refusal attacked Copenhagen, the capital of Denmark.

1. **Nelson** was in the forefront of the attack. It was here that the traditional episode occurred of his putting a telescope to his blind eye, and thus pretending not to see the recall signal issued by his less confident superior, Parker.

10. **leviathans**: a vague term, used for marine monsters, generally whales.

63. **Elsinore** (Helsingfors) is a fort commanding the approach by sea to Copenhagen. It is the scene of Shakespeare's *Hamlet*.

67. **Riou** was the name of a captain killed in the battle.

Thomas Campbell (1777—1844) is now chiefly remembered by two or three songs of war, including this one and *Ye Mariners of England* (see p. 162). They are noticeable on account of their original metres, cleverly managed by the poet.

CHARACTER OF THE HAPPY WARRIOR.

Wordsworth himself says that this poem, which does not specifically refer to Nelson, was inspired by the thought of him. It was written in 1806; Nelson died at the battle of Trafalgar on 21 October, 1805.

4. Notice **real** is two syllables, which is the proper pronunciation, and formerly was always used.

19, 20. **to abate her feeling**, to become callous.

29. This means 'where men are tempted to guard against ill by evil measures, and (l. 31) even what they do well, or to a good end, is based on wrong, he (the Happy Warrior) bases good on good.'

43. **they** means 'wealth and honours.'

59. **bias**: a metaphor from the game of bowls. The bowls contain a weight, which makes them roll not in a straight line.

68. **toward**, favourable.

85. The whole poem consists of two sentences.

William Wordsworth (1770—1850), poet laureate 1843—1850 (succeeding Southey, see notes on *After Blenheim*, p. 206), is usually put with Coleridge at the head of the literary revolt from artificiality and the 'return to nature' which marked the close of the eighteenth century. Unequal in his poetry, he occasionally attained the heights of true inspiration and poetic diction, and is always an interesting and stimulating poet to read.

YE MARINERS OF ENGLAND.

Another fine song of Thomas Campbell's (see notes on *The Battle of the Baltic*). It was founded on a seventeenth-century song, beginning:

> You gentlemen of England
> Who live at home at ease.

Again notice the fine effect produced by Campbell's ingenious variation of the pause in the seventh line of each verse.

6. This probably refers to Russia's declaration of war in 1807.

15. **Blake** destroyed a fleet of Spain in the harbour of Teneriffe, in the Canary Islands, 20 April, 1657. He died in the same year, but not in battle.

THE BURIAL OF SIR JOHN MOORE AT CORUNNA.

Sir John Moore, in the winter of 1808—9, was driven into the north-west corner of Spain by Marshals Soult and Ney, acting under Napoleon's instructions 'to drive him into the sea.' He stood at bay at Corunna on the coast, waiting for ships to take his army off. They arrived on 15 January, 1809, and Moore embarked all but the soldiers. The next day the French attacked in force, but were repulsed, though Moore lost his life.

2. It was Moore's own wish to be buried where he fell.

9. No coffin could be procured.

27. The burial-party were alarmed by firing at about eight in the morning.

Charles Wolfe (1791—1823), an obscure Irish clergyman, wrote this famous poem at some time between 1812 and 1815 while at Trinity College, Dublin. It is remarkable not only for its own merit, but for the facts that Wolfe wrote hardly anything else, and that the authorship was claimed by and attributed to a number of people, including Lord Byron.

WATERLOO.

1. The poem opens with a description of the Duchess of Richmond's ball at Brussels, Belgium's capital, and Wellington's headquarters, on 15 June, 1815. The Duke attended the ball, though he knew of Napoleon's advance, in order to prevent any alarm being given.

18. There was no fighting on this night, nor till the next day; so this description is imaginary.

20. Brunswick's fated chieftain, the Duke of Brunswick was killed at Quatre Bras on the 16th.

46—7. The Camerons were the 79th Regiment; Albyn's hills means the Highlands.

54. Donald Cameron of Lochiel was in the Jacobite rebellion of 1745.

68. As a matter of fact, the battles of Ligny and Quatre Bras on the 16th preceded the great battle of Waterloo on the 18th.

George Gordon Byron, Lord Byron (1788—1824), in a short, brilliant, and merry life, gained an immense audience, and supplied it with a novel form of romantic verse-tales and dramas. Only at the end of his career did he find his true medium, the original and lively medley *Don Juan*, infinitely his greatest contribution to literature.

ENGLAND'S DEAD.

9. This refers to an expedition sent in 1801 to Egypt to drive out the French army.

39. Roncesvalles, in the Pyrenees, where Charlemagne is recorded to have fought the Moors. One of many engagements between French and English in 1813 took place on the same spot.

VICTORIA'S TEARS.

Queen Victoria succeeded to the throne of England on the death of William IV in 1837.

4. all other: *i.e.* all other majesty.

Elizabeth Barrett Browning (1806—1861), wife of the poet Robert Browning, was gifted with true poetical intuition and imagination, but her poems are often hampered by her lack of a musical ear and of range of expression. Nevertheless she is easily the first of English women poets.

ODE ON THE DEATH OF THE DUKE OF WELLINGTON.

The Duke of Wellington died on 14 September, 1852. The poem was written within a week of his death, an extraordinary feat, considering the high level to which it attains.

9. He was buried in St Paul's Cathedral (see l. 49), beside Nelson.

15. Representatives of every European army attended the funeral, as well as of every British regiment.

30. Wellington's life falls into two parts, the first military, the second political.

42. *i.e.* the conqueror of Napoleon.

80—2. Supposed to be spoken by Nelson, the 'mighty Seaman.'

99. Wellington's first victory was at the battle of Assaye in 1803, when with four or five thousand men he routed 60,000 Mahrattas.

101—118. Wellington's methods and success in the Peninsular War are commemorated in these lines. Between 1809 and 1814 he drove the French northwards from Lisbon and beyond the Pyrenees.

119—133. Napoleon, banished to Elba in 1814, returned in 1815, but after a reign of two or three months was finally defeated by Wellington on Sunday ('that loud Sabbath') 18 June, 1815, in 'that world-earthquake, Waterloo.'

197. horn: the *cornucopia*, or horn of plenty.

229. He was popularly called 'The Iron Duke.'

Alfred, Lord Tennyson (1809—1892), poet laureate in succession to Wordsworth from 1850 till his death, was writing poetry the whole of his life, and, unlike many poets, continually improving. He created a new and most musical form of blank verse, wrote many beautiful lyrics, and throughout handled his native language with care and success.

THE CHARGE OF THE LIGHT BRIGADE.

Immediately after the Charge of the Heavy Brigade, an order arrived from Lord Raglan, the commander-in-chief, that the cavalry, under Lord Cardigan, were to recover certain guns that had been abandoned earlier in the day. The officer who brought the order was killed, and it has never been resolved who was to blame for the 'blunder' (l. 12).

38. Only about half the 600 returned. The episode illustrates a not unparalleled feature of British warfare, a blunder of organisation counterbalanced by personal gallantry, individual or collective. The famous phrase 'C'est magnifique, mais ce n'est pas la guerre,' said to have been used on this occasion by a French general, sums up the situation neatly.

For EU product safety concerns, contact us at Calle de José Abascal, 56–1°, 28003 Madrid, Spain or eugpsr@cambridge.org.

www.ingramcontent.com/pod-product-compliance
Ingram Content Group UK Ltd.
Pitfield, Milton Keynes, MK11 3LW, UK
UKHW012331130625
459647UK00009B/209